Voice of a Southern Boy

DOUG BREWER

Doug Brewer

Dedicated to my loving wife, Lynn, my son, Douglas, all my family and all my friends.

Table of Contents

Chapter 1	1
Chapter 2	8
Chapter 3	22
Chapter 4	29
Chapter 5	45
Chapter 6	65
Chapter 7	77
Chapter 8	100
Chapter 9	107
Chapter 10	134
Chapter 11	141

Doug Brewer

Chapter 1

Three year old me, Howenwald Tennessee

On a cool spring morning at eight thirty a.m., I was born on Eagle Creek in Wayne County, Tennessee. The year was 1943 and although World War II impacted the rest of the world outside our rural, poverty-stricken community, the only impact it would have for me was my namesake. I was named after General Douglas MacArthur and my grandfather on my mother's side. I was the seventh child born to my parents and just missed being born on my father's birthday by one day.

The modern conveniences being made available to others in the world hadn't quite made it to rural Middle Tennessee at the time, where the main source of income was cutting timber or moonshining. My dad cut timber and he may or may not have been involved with moonshine. It seemed that everyone was involved in the illegal but booming business of moonshine, either brewing it up, guarding the still, or selling it.

Timber cutters made maybe twenty dollars a week. We, like the other country folks around us, had to grow our own vegetables, tend to cows for butter and milk, and raise chickens and hogs for eggs and meat. Nothing was wasted. Even the fat from the hogs was cooked down and used for lard and making cracklings.

Things were rough all over. All the folks around us were as poor as we were. With seven mouths to feed on twenty dollars a week, I guess our first venture was to move to Arkansas for a short time. I can't remember much about that. My family talked a lot about how bad the water was. We were used to the spring water, clean, clear and cool. We didn't stay long in Arkansas and moved back to Middle Tennessee where all our kin folks were.

My parents had been from the same county so all my family members were in one place. Soon after we moved back, my baby brother was born. For the last four years, I had been the baby of the family, but I don't recall any special treatment. I do recall my two older sisters kidding me about not being the baby anymore. I remember throwing rocks at them over it. Where we lived, you could reach down anywhere and find good rocks for throwing. The old timers would say, "If it don't stick, sting or bite, it's a rock."

Although the water was pristine and quenching, we had to walk a half mile to get water to take up to the house. We had a path down to the spring, which was in the very bottom of a "holler." Basically, a holler (slang for hollow) was a valley of sorts nestled between two hills.

My brother Brownie, the one closest to my age, was always trying to make money. He would let me go with him so we could cover both sides of the road as we looked for whiskey bottles that had been tossed out of car windows. There were moonshiners all around who would buy the discarded bottles to package their moonshine. It's funny to me now that this was actually one of the first forms of recycling. My brother got three cents for pint bottles and two cents for half pint bottles. He always sold these to a moonshiner who had a wooden leg. He had a still upon a creek close to his house. The creek ran just past the shiner's front porch and the water was good and clear for making moonshine. You could see the smoke from his still. Back then shiners used wood. Nowadays, they use propane.

When we got enough bottles to sell, it would be my job to wash them. Brownie always got the money and I don't remember him sharing it with me. We carried the bottles in a tow sack. If we didn't find any bottles, my brother would sell his own bottles back to the moonshiner.

My brother would make money by hook or crook. I guess he used the money to go to the show. My older brother watched a still for someone once. He had to be on the lookout for the "revenuers." The Feds would come in and break up a man's still and if The Shiner got caught, he went to prison. He was dating a woman who had a car so she would pick him up to go on dates.

My younger brother, Hubert, would mow yards, dig up bushes, and do just about anything that needed doing to make money. One time he took on a job clearing a large field with only a grubbing hoe and an axe. He worked all summer. This would have been hard work for an able-bodied man, so it was especially taxing for a skinny young boy. Just like my brother Brownie, Hubert wasn't one to share his earnings either.

Years later, Brownie did let me drive his cars and he would give me spending money. He was always there to protect me. We were close. He didn't let anyone pick on me. Once I was going to school way out in the country where the schoolhouse was close to a farmer's house who had horses and an electric fence. Our school was heated with coal and had a huge coal bin. The buses ran more than one route and we were on the earlier one, so we got to school first. We used to play outside until the bus came back after the second route. There was a bully (yes, we had bullies back in those days, too) who would pick a new target every single day. Of course, he would choose one of us smaller boys. He would take an undeserving boy by the ear and grab the fences. It would be enough to knock your socks off! He did this to me one day, so I told Brownie.

He didn't say anything other than, "I will handle it." The next day the bully came up to me and grabbed me by the ear. As we got close to the fence I squirmed to get away. I didn't know my brother was in the coal shed waiting for the right moment. He came out with a huge lump of coal and smashed it against the thug's head. He went down and my brother disappeared. I will always remember the triumph I felt when that coal shattered. I still see it clearly in my mind. The bully never knew what hit him, but I don't recall him ever mistreating anyone else.

We had an uncle that lived across from us and every Saturday when he came from town he would be feeling no pain (probably from the shine). He would bring me a piece of bubble gum. As he walked down the lane to his house he would yell out to me, "Hey, little soldier boy!" I never knew why he called me this, but I loved to hear those words because it meant a piece of bubble gum. I couldn't wait for him to come home! I would run full speed to get my treat. The trek was a little downhill and sometimes I would get so eager I would fall and skin my knees. The sweetness of the gum made me forget about the pain in my knees. Why he chose me of all my brothers and sisters to give me the gum, I will never know. I was always as grateful as if he had given me a new bike. Rest his soul.

I can remember going with the older ones to pack water. We were always barefoot in the summer time. As soon as the weather got warm the shoes would come off until the first frost came again. Once when we were going for water I was running along in front of the path. The path was very narrow and I stepped on a snake. I can still feel it slithering with its scaly coldness. I probably didn't weigh forty pounds at the time.

Early one summer morning, a neighbor came down this same narrow path calling out to my mom. He delivered the news that her father, my grandfather, had passed away. I recall how my mother was so hurt. She was crying and I never could stand to see my mother cry. If she cried, I cried, too. I didn't understand the full impact but I still cried the whole day when he was buried. My oldest brother, Odie, tried to calm me down. I had never been to a funeral. I remember that folks kept talking about his coffin, but what I heard was "coffee." I saw a pile of dirt with an old shag carpet thrown over it. I had it in my head that this dirt was coffee grounds. As they started shoveling the dirt over the coffin, I couldn't understand why they were covering him up with coffee grounds. I was four years old and even though I laugh about it now, I know we were sheltered in a way that kids aren't sheltered now.

My mother would cry from time to time when she thought about her father. There wasn't much time for her to mourn with a household to run and the full-time job of looking after her family. The days were long and just seemed to drag. The heat was unpardonable in the summer with the sun beating down on our house that had no electricity. The only air we got was from a merciful breeze and that didn't happen very often.

Brownie was old enough to go visit with the aunts and uncles and other extended family. One spring morning he had gone to spend the weekend with an uncle of ours who fished a lot. Because it turned out to be colder than expected that Saturday morning, my uncle and brother didn't go. However, one of my cousins and some more boys went down to the Buffalo River to mess around and kill time. There were kids on both sides of the river and my cousin was trying to swim from one side to the other. He went down under the water and didn't come back up. He drowned. The news traveled to us pretty quickly. My mother was crying because she thought it was my brother who had drowned. The messenger had said it was one of the Brewer boys who had just drowned in the Buffalo River. Mama knew this was where my uncle and brother had planned to go fish. She was relieved it wasn't her son, but she grieved a different grief for the mother who did lose a son. He had been only seventeen and had a twin sister. That was a sad time.

I don't remember visiting my mom's mother after her father, who we called Pappy, died but we did go visit my father's parents. My Pa was a mean, cold man, but my Ma was a very special person. She was almost full-blooded Indian. She wore dresses down to her work shoes that I always thought looked like men's shoes. She was a quiet and humble person. She could cook the best bacon and biscuits I ever tasted. She always had chickens. She would save her eggs and when the drummer came by once a week, she traded the eggs for snuff or whatever he had on the truck that she wanted. I don't think she ever went to town. During our visits on Saturday nights we would all listen to the Grand Ole Opry on a battery-powered radio. Sometimes Maw would dance for us. I can still see her pull that long dress up just above her shoes and dance. We thought she was so funny.

My folks, Arie and Roxie Brewer mid 50's

Chapter 2

The Family: Brownie, Ludine, Mama (holding Bernice), Odie, and Daddy (holding Rosetta)

There was a movement in the late forties of families moving to West Tennessee to pick and chop cotton. The farmers had figured out that most of the families were large and the bigger the family, the more labor the farmer could get. The farmers would send trucks and a couple of farm hands to move the families to West Tennessee. Our family, like a lot of others at the time, agreed to move down there. We were all packed and ready to go one summer morning when a truck pulled up. The driver got out and the passenger followed. I couldn't believe it! The man was black. I had never seen a black person before. I didn't know if I should run from this stranger or what. Anyway, we got loaded up and headed to what would later be known as the hometown of Carl Perkins, Mr. Blue Suede Shoes, in Tiptonville, Tennessee.

It wasn't long before we were picking cotton with our neighbors, white folks and black folks alike. There was no difference in the fields. It was just work, but when we went to town the black folks went in different directions than the white folks. I couldn't understand this at all. I was unaware of what was going on, but I knew that wasn't right.

I loved working with the black folks. We had some great, fun times. I loved to hear the black workers sing. No one and I mean no one could sing like those we called "colored" folks. The way those sounds stirred my soul has never been repeated and you truly would have had to have been there to have felt what I felt.

I had never been out of Middle Tennessee until going to chop cotton in Tiptonville. This was a huge adjustment for a five-year-old kid. It was an adjustment for our whole family. Our income went from fifteen to twenty dollars a week to twenty dollars a day. This was more money than my family could have previously imagined on the farm. A bus would come around on Saturday to take folks to town to get groceries and to relax.

One Saturday someone took me to a show. I had never been to a show. The movie was Tarzan and I remember it well. During one scene, a lion was chasing the natives. As the lion ran towards what would have been the camera, it looked to my young eyes like he was running into the theater. I took off. Color me gone.

Another time I went into the grocery store and found the biggest orange ever. I got it and ran to the park where my sisters, Berniece and Rosetta, were playing. I bragged, "Look, I got me a big orange with my money!" They made so much fun of me for that. I had mistaken a grapefruit for an orange. The only time we had seen fruit was at Christmas time when we would go to the courthouse and fruit would be passed out to the poor families. We would get oranges, apples, orange candy slices, a few pieces of hard candy, and two or three nuts.

Summer had come and gone quickly and fall was about to be over when my dad decided to move us back to Wayne County. He just never did adjust to making that kind of money. When we were preparing to move back, my dad went out and bought a car he didn't know how to drive. He had the dealer bring it to him. The man tried to show him how to operate it, but Daddy was too embarrassed about not being able to drive so he just let the dealer show him the starter and clutch and how to shift. Then he left. There was a field in front of our house that had bushes that were all grown up. Let's just say that soon after Daddy started "driving," there were no bushes anymore. I can still hear the grinding of the gears and buck jumping that car was tough. We had to hide and laugh at him or he would have beaten the crap out of us.

I started to school that fall of 1949. I hated school with all my being. We always took our lunch in a paper sack. It usually consisted of eggs and biscuits and sometimes a little bacon, just whatever was left from breakfast. Of course, we had to use the same sack over and over.

There was some kind of school program that allowed us to get a bottle of milk for free. It was embarrassing to me. The way that was done by the school was all wrong. It was already too easy to separate the haves and have-nots simply by their lunches. The ones of us that took our lunches didn't sit with the ones who had plate lunches. The upper-class kids made fun of us and this caused me to hate to go to school. That sparked a flame in me that is still there today. Nothing ruffles my feathers faster today, as it has throughout my life, than seeing people looked down on because of what they don't have.

I think that flame has served me well though. I worked as soon as I got big enough. I didn't want to ask anyone for anything. By the next year we moved back to West Tennessee for Daddy to try his hand at prosperity again. By the time I was ten years old I had gone from picking cotton to chopping cotton, a job unheard of for a ten year old at the time. I have continued to work throughout my life and will continue to do so until it just isn't possible.

I wouldn't trade my experiences growing up for anything. It was a hard life with no indoor plumbing, no electricity, and taking baths in a number two washtub. This was the South, hard and hot.

Before long, we moved right back to cotton country, into the house we had left before winter. I was anxious to see my friends. There were always lots of kids in the houses up and down the lane. Our neighbor even had a television set, the only one around at the time. We were allowed to watch the television on Saturday mornings until noon. There were Westerns on every Saturday morning. The lady of the house was a sweet person who would always clean her house on Saturday, but she would wait until noon before she urged us out with her declaration of, "I gotta clean the house. Y'all go on out now and play."

With the Westerns we had watched still fresh on our minds, we would usually go play cowboys and Indians for the rest of the day. We amused ourselves in ways that kids today can't imagine. We would have fun just rolling an old tire around or riding a stick horse.

Doug Brewer

One thing I remember clearly about my Southern childhood is the church revivals. Buses would run and pick folks up. We would pack those buses and have some real barn burners back then. I always felt like the preacher was looking right at me and talking especially to me. I know I made a few fingerprints on a pew or two. I guess I was guilty of something or at least I thought I was. There were always baptisms that followed the revivals because there would be several that had claimed salvation during the services. Since we were close to beautiful Reelfoot Lake, this was where most of the baptisms took place, snakes and all. At that time there were three beaches in Lake County and within ten miles we had the mighty Mississippi.

I remember getting my first black eye along a Mississippi river bank. I was showing Berniece how to cast when fishing in the river. You had to use heavy weights. She went to cast out and hit me with the weights. Thank heavens she didn't hook me but I wore that shiner for weeks. Sisters can be rough on their younger brothers and vice versa.

One time my sister was writing to this boy during the days of actually communicating through the mail. She had been diligently waiting for the mailman to bring a letter from her sweetheart. My dad could not know about this. She was pretty sweet on this fella, and I thought it would be a good idea to intercept the letter before she could get to it and make her wait a little longer. She took a little red rocking chair and hit me with the rockers. I gave her the letter after I got my breath back.

Life was so much better back then. I would go fishing every day or just go running through the woods playing. I always had a homemade slingshot. I was pretty good with it but I was no Slingshot Charlie. I did shoot a bird flying one time, just pure luck. I killed lots of lizards and snakes with it, though. I carried a slingshot all the time when I was really young or until my brother, Odie, went to Michigan and started to work for Ford Motor Company. He came home on vacation once and he brought me a BB gun. Man, I was uptown with this thing! I threw my sling shot away.

Birds, snakes, and lizards were far and few between after I had had it for a while, but I also made a big mistake. I hid out in the bushes and of all people, the brother who bought the gun for me just happened to walk by. I shot him in the leg. That ended my BB gun. He took it away from me.

Later on, Odie brought me a bicycle with two tubeless tires on it. Yes, tubeless tire. After I had a flat tire, I found out you couldn't find replacement tires for it. Nevertheless, being one to not be put down, I put sawdust in the tire. I packed it with all I could and put water on the sawdust to make it swell up and it worked for a while.

Then, I rode it on the rims until I wore them out. On one of my brother's trips home, he had driven a late-model Buick he had just purchased. He had a wreck only a few miles from being home. He tore his car up but no one was hurt. As I am writing this, I have to say it still puzzles me as to why he was so good to me. He had three step children he should have been buying things for. And I also realize I'm not sure if I ever let him know how much it meant to me.

The creeks and springs in Middle Tennessee were a big part of my childhood life. I would play in the cold, untainted fresh water, catching small fish and finding arrowheads in the creek beds. When we lived close to my cousins, we would always play and swim in the creeks. The water was always cold because the creeks were fed by springs. We would keep our milk and butter in the cold water of the springs. We always kept our spring cleaned out and deep so the water would be colder. We would play, get hot, and run to the spring and lie down and drink from the spring. I don't know if I could do that now. Today if I were to drink that refreshing, pure water on a hot day, I would probably get so beside myself I would choke up. When I think of things that have changed over the years as the world has gotten more progressive, that water makes me realize there are some things you can't perfect.

Snakes were common where we lived. Once we were picking blackberries. Berniece and I were picking together. She was always afraid of her own shadow. I saw this snake crawling in the briers. This was one massive snake. I told her, "Snake!" She thought I was playing so I went to the same side she was on so the snake would go out the other way. Sure enough, it crawled out. I called my dad. He came over and took rocks and killed him. He had several rattles and was six feet long. The gentleman who let us pick blackberries told us there were no rattlesnakes in the area. So, dad tied him to the bumper and pulled him up to the gate of the man's house. He came out and said, "You didn't pick very many berries that quick." He shook his head.

Dad said, "Come here. We'll give you your share." He came over and saw the snake and his eyes widened in disbelief. He said, "Just keep all the berries." We said our goodbyes and left him the rattler.

I always was trying to make some money. I sold garden seed for two or three springs and tried selling salve. I can't remember the name but it was clear, like Vaseline. When I was selling seed, there was some kind of contest sponsored by the company to win a trip to North Dakota to an Indian reservation. I wanted to win that trip so badly. Well, I got a letter saying I won, but you had to furnish money for this and that so that was the end of my dreams of traveling for the time being.

As I got a little older, things were better. We were like everyone else. We worked farms and our incomes were basically the same. School wasn't that bad anymore. And all of a sudden, the girls had started to look good. Everybody had sweethearts. Back in the day in school, you'd pass notes to each other. Not very many people had phone in their homes, so notes and letters were a prime form of communication. All notes were SWAK (sealed with a kiss). One of my sweethearts always signed I'm yours until the Mississippi River wears rubber pants to keep its bottom dry. I had lots of sweethearts between then and the time my wife came along.

I guess I was like most Southern boys in the fifties. We were rebels. Whatever our parents wanted, we wanted the opposite. That wasn't indicative of our time, it's the way it always has been and always will be. However, my mother was my strength. She had the most intuitive insight. As I grew older, those simple things she told me are important today. Some of her sayings were as follows: if the lord wills..., do not put off tomorrow what you can do today, mind your manners, do not disrespect women, always give a day's labor for a day's wages, and lots more.

If she asked me to do something, I would procrastinate. I would tell her I would do it later. Women back then didn't get the credit they deserved. Most worked way before daylight until well after dark. My mother was no exception, but she took it in stride. She cooked over a hot wood cook stove. She washed clothes, cleaned house, and then went to the field and worked all day just like we did. But she never got to sit down when we got home until all of us were fed and the dishes were washed. Every morning she would get up at the crack of dawn and start all over. If you're reading this book and your mom is still living, stop right now. Close the cover and go see her or at least call her. Just a simple, "Mom, I was thinking about you, I really appreciate and love you, or thanks for all you do." It won't hurt you, do it.

One of my true treasures are my old friends. I don't see some of them very much, but they mean a lot to me. Some of them are ones I grew up with. I try to maintain relationships with my friends and we go out to eat and go on vacation together. One of my dearest and loving friends lost her husband a few years back. We try to spend time with her. I have always loved her as a friend. I don't believe we have ever had a cross word. We all need friends. I would hate to look back on my life and say that I never had friends. I miss those long, hot summer days just hanging with my friends.

We would walk most places we went. We would walk for two to three miles to an old country store just to get a Coca Cola and sit around talking. Some of my fondest memories were of just hanging around town. Some of my girlfriends worked in the café where all teenagers hung out. I would give them a ride home. Just before time to close, two of the girls there would fix me a cheeseburger and fries. Oh, they were so good. Not because they took care of the cost, but they really did taste better back then. I will never forget those friends. Words were never spoken about paying. They would fix the food and come and get the plate. One of them has since passed on. I loved her as a sister. I remember later in life as she was sick, we were at a reunion at Reelfoot Lake. I danced with her for the last time. The song "Until A Tear Becomes a Rose" was playing. She spoke softly, "I have had many a tear and not one has become a rose." I never saw her again until her funeral. She is thought of often.

It seems I was always getting into something. My grandmother dipped snuff. It seems like all grandmothers dipped. I decided one day I would get me some of her snuff and run all the way to the shed where no one could see me. When no one was watching, I ran to get it as fast as I could and I was out of breath. I grabbed the snuff. My breath was labored from all the running, but I got a pinch and persevered. Well, when I got it close to my mouth, I sucked some of the dust into my throat. I got so strangled, I lost my breath and got sick. No more snuff for me!

Tobacco was a vice for folks to pass the time in the day. It was a staple as much as beans or potatoes. Brownie smoked. I stole some of his cigarettes, crawled under the floor, and lit me one up. I was puffing away, not knowing the smoke was coming out. Brownie saw the smoke. Well my brother-in-law, nicknamed Boots, smoked cigars. Boots was married to my sister, Ludene. Anyway, they got together and took me with them down the road. They did not tell on me. We walked together down the road.

Boots got out some cigars, lit them up and said. "Hey, you want one? Here, light up. You're big enough to smoke." They both demonstrated how to puff. "Now, suck the smoke down. Inhale," they coached me. Well, I got so sick I must have turned blue. They took the cigar from me. Needless to say, I didn't want to smoke for a long time.

The next thing they did was took me snip hunting. Well, if you've never been, you missed it. They managed to talk me into going one night. They really talked this snip hunting up. They told me I was to hold a sack open and sit really still. The plan was for them to go down the ditch and drive them to me and I was instructed to close the sack real quick. I waited forever. Well, they didn't show up nor did a snip. No snips, imagine that. They are still laughing about that one.

Then, they took me on a coon hunt. I thought the dogs were supposed to chase the coons. Well, we ran through the woods all night over logs, through swamps and briers. Finally, we sat down on a log. Brownie took out a bottle of peach brandy. That alcohol smelled so good. Somehow, we finally treed a coon. Through the excitement, my brother broke his bottle of peach brandy. Well, we smelled peach brandy throughout the woods the rest of the night. That was my first and last coon hunt. I was fonder of hunting rabbits, squirrels, and ducks. Once, my friend Tommy and me were going rabbit hunting. Tommy's dad, a World War 2 vet, was a good man. We enjoyed being around him. He was this kind of man. He asked if he could go with us. We told him, "Sure."

He came out of the house with a 22 rifle. I said, "Where do you think you're going with that rifle?"

He said, "This is all I need."

I said, "I will carry all you kill with that." Well, by the end of the day, me and Tommy were carrying all we could. Never mess with a WW2 vet, especially when it comes to his ability to kill rabbits with a rifle.

On one of our squirrel hunts, my dad was walking through tall weeds to get into the woods. Someone had already been through there. They had made a path. I was behind my dad. I was looking down because I was looking for snakes. He was already looking through the trees to see if any squirrels were moving. As I scoured the ground for snakes, I noticed that whoever had traipsed through the weeds before us had knocked down a huge wasp nest.

As I went to push my dad aside, he saw it and jumped to the right. Well, when I missed him, my force caused me to fall right into that angry nest. They covered me up. I was hurting so bad, I got down on the ground. Well, I was making it worse. Every time I rolled on one, he stung me again. Another hunter, Jimmy, was close by. He told my dad to bring me over to him. He chewed tobacco, so he had me take my shirt off and he covered me up with tobacco juice.

It felt like it was drawing my skin. He and my dad kept chewing more tobacco. I started to get a little sick. I think it was the tobacco juice that made me sick. When I got home one of my neighbors had washed all the juice off me and bathed me with alcohol.

One other time I was with our neighbor riding around on Sunday afternoon. My friend Tommy's dad was driving and we had all the windows down. There were no air conditioners in the car back then. As we were driving, I was by the window. We met a car. This is where I got my second black eye. As we met the car, someone throw out a pecan. It hit me right under my eye. A half an inch higher and I would've been called One Eye Jack. My eye stayed black for days. I don't remember what we did with the pecan. If someone ate it, I hope it was good.

Where we lived, ducks would leave the lake in the afternoon and fill the corn fields up feeding. I would go rabbit hunting and as the ducks started coming into the fields, I would sit down on the fence row and sometimes I would get a shot. I didn't have a duck stamp so I was always looking for the game warden.

One day, ducks were coming in so I just got up against the fence with vines on it. I was small. It didn't take much to hide me. Well, I was waiting and I was NERVOUS because I didn't have a stamp. Shooting up the way from me a few minutes later, WHAM. A duck had been hit. The wounded fowl fell and hit the fence behind me. I almost jumped out of my skin. I got me a duck and never fired a shot. Pretty good, right?

Another day I was walking around hunting and the ducks started flying. I thought I could never get close to them by the fence. So, I thought to myself: let me see, why don't I just get me some corn stalks and lie down, cover myself, and when the ducks light and start feeding, I would jump up and shoot among them. Well, what I didn't know is that someone had built a duck blind beside the side of the field.

Well, I get covered up to wait on the ducks. Meanwhile, the hunters came and got into their blind. I didn't know they were there and they didn't know I was lying down in the field. As the ducks were circling above me, I was waiting for them to land, but duck hunters shoot them in the air when they're low enough. As I was watching, they were getting lower and lower. About that time, BANG, BANG! Ducks and shots were falling all around me. I jumped up hollering, scared to death. Well, I ran all the way home. No more makeshift duck blinds for me. I don't know what happened to the hunters. They were running, too, the last I looked. I don't think they had permission to hunt. The farmer's wife didn't allow any hunting. She knew I did anyway. I can still hear her shouting "Stop that shooting up there!" I never did answer her.

Coincidentally, I knew her as she was not only a real fine lady, but a school teacher. I should have listened to her about a lot of things. As I look back, she wanted the best for me, always gave the best advice, but I was too young to know what I needed.

Chapter 3

This was a specific time in my life when I was really growing up. Where we lived now, there were several boys and girls up and down the roads. We became friends. Some closer than others and in the country, we played outside. We were always outside. Parent didn't have to worry about you like they do now. We stayed out until ten o clock. Nothing was wrong about that.

One of the best sources of entertainment for us was the drive-in theater. We lived about three miles from the nearest drive-in. The drive-in had a huge row of wild rose bushes around the whole thing, except right around the concession stand, where there was an opening about five feet wide. It was about one hundred yards from the concession stand. Me and my friends would walk over and wait until dark. The manager knew people were slipping into the drive-in and he would watch out the back door. From time to time, we would watch him and as soon as he looked and walked away from the door, we would run in and start walking up to cars like we belonged there so he wouldn't think anything. The drive-in had chairs in front of the concession stand so you could sit outside your car if you wanted to. We would go one at a time and go sit down.

One night we got in and were sitting watching the movie. My friends had little brothers, so this night one followed us. As the manager was already eyeing us, my friend's brother came over with a big smile, proud of himself, says "Ha! I slipped in, too!" Well, we all got thrown out.

One time on the way home, we stopped to use an outhouse. They all had tin roofs. As we were sitting in the quiet of the night, someone threw rocks on top of the outhouse. They say white boys can't run. Well, you would disagree if you saw us that night.

I might have mentioned that farmers had workers from Mexico who came in on visas to work the crops. Well, on one night we decided to go to the drive-in so we got over to the edge behind the rose bushes early. There were beans planted this year. I guess the beans were three feet tall. Well, while we were waiting for it to get dark, unbeknownst to us, some of the Mexicans had come through the beans in behind us. We didn't know they were there, and they didn't know we were there. And as always, we waited until the manager looked out and walked back inside. We would always run in when the coast was clear. Well, just as we were ready, apparently our Mexican neighbors knew the same trick. So, when he went inside, the Mexicans jumped up, ran over us, and just as they scared the life out of us, we scared the Mexicans also. We were running in every direction. I don't know what they were saying. It was like a covey of quails, flushing and sounding like a cock pheasant coming up.

Eventually, we found new ways to slip into the drive-in. We had an older friend who had an old car. He would drive and someone else would have to hold the gear shift to keep it in gear. We fixed the backseat so we could push it out, so in the trunk we would go. As soon as we were parked away from the concession stand, we pushed the backseat out and climbed out. Home free. Another clever way we would slip in would be using the poodle skirts girls were wearing back in the fifties. No, we didn't wear them. Well, I would sit in the floor with one girl on one side and one girl on the other side. They had me covered. I was perched, perfectly hidden between the two girls. I know what you're thinking and you can just stop. It was clean fun and it was always a rush to beat the system. As you went in paid and got your speaker, they would always look inside your car to try to catch us sneaky kids.

It was fun, the things we did. I remember in all this growing up thing, I found my first love. That first puppy love is a powerful thing and the one who stole my heart the first time has always been a special person in my life.

As we were working in the fields picking cotton, me and Hubert would sing. The Everley brothers were popular at the time so we would sing their songs. We must have done pretty good. The folks in the field would ask us to sing all the time. If we sang "Wake up Little Susie" once, we did it a hundred times over. On Saturdays we would get together at the home of one of the neighbors. The girls always danced. We would eat hamburgers and our days just flew by.

We all grew up and some of us moved away, but all the good times are still as fresh in my mind as if they happened yesterday. I think the people you meet as you're growing up are special and these bonds are never broken. I still have some of these people in my life. We were friends as we grew up and we still are.

On some of the long hot summer days, we would slip off and go swimming in ponds and gravel pits. Our days were filled with fun and laughter. Growing up was like this in the South. No money, no swimming pools, but there was life that most people missed. This is something that can't be bought. Money doesn't give you this kind of life and memories.

We needed this fun in the worst way because our farm life was hard. We worked in the cotton and bean fields from before sunrise to sunset. These were hot, long days for very little money, but we got by. You have to be from the South to understand. I was always trying to be more than just a laborer. Soon, I went from using a hoe handle, chopping cotton, to driving a farm tractor. This was much easier.

The thing I hated most on the farm was to see my mom have to labor just as hard as us and still do the housework. As I've said, my mom was a special person and was the hardest working woman I ever saw. I give my mom all the credit for what I have accomplished in my life. She set the example for life. She was always encouraging me, teaching me right from wrong. All good things in my life were passed through to me by my loving, caring, God-fearing mom.

When we lived in this one area, we had several families living close by. There were hills and some gullies and we would all get together and play in the gullies at night, hiding from one another. We would choose teams and play army, boys and girls alike. Some might have stolen a kiss or two now and then. We were at the age where we starting to be inquisitive.

One night, one of the girls yells out "Oh my leg! I think I broke my leg!" Well, we were a long way from her house. Me and my best friend toted her all the way home. When she reached her yard gate, she took off running, laughing all the way. We were exhausted because of her, but we couldn't help but laugh with her. This was our kind of fun.

One day we were down the road and a beer truck stopped at the local store. One of the boys somehow got some beer off the truck. We went up to our swimming hole and popped the top. We drank the beer. We were feeling the effects right away. I learned you don't drink hot beer through a straw unless you want a buzz real quick. We were all laughing and having a big time. Everybody wondered what was wrong with us but we weren't talking.

One night we took a lady's purse and laid it in the middle of the road. We tied a fishing line to it, and as cars would come by, they would see it and stop. By the time they got back to where it was, we pulled it back into the ditch. Sometimes, they would talk to themselves. It was hard not to laugh out loud. I know this has been around a long time. I don't know where we came up with these crazy ideas. It would just be something to do, another night of growing up in the South.

I got my first car about this time, a 1949 Ford coupe, three speed on the tree. You had to hold the gear stick to keep it in low gear. I saved every penny I could get my hands on to buy it. I paid 75 dollars for it. This car changed everything for me. I found out real quick that if you had a car in our neighborhood, you went from being a nobody to the most popular boy in town. All the boys were suddenly my best friends and as I soon found out, girls started taking a serious look at me. With a car, it was nothing to find a date every Saturday night. We would go riding around and, of course, we would go to the trusty drive-in. None of us had any money but we would pool our money for gas and on Wednesday nights we could get a whole car load in for a dollar. There was nothing like these summer nights in the South.

Left to right: Jean Robinson Lamb, Margie Lemons Pugh, and Judy Hollingsworth Cruce.

Left to right: Me, Margie Lemons, James Williams, Judy Hollingsworth, Lynn Robinson, Penny Gale Kemp, and Jimmy Williams

Left to right: Me, Jerry Robinson, Lynn Robinson, my baby brother, Hubert, Jimmy Williams, and James Williams.

Chapter 4

Things started to change for us as we went from being boys to young men. James Dean, Elvis, and other rebels were on the scene. I guess we started to rebel also, getting a little wild. One night me and my best friend went to a basketball game. His brother drove us and he and his date went riding around. He was to pick us up around ten p.m. His girlfriend had to be home by eleven, and we were thirty miles away from where she lived. Well, it was late when they returned to pick us up, so my friend was driving fast to get his girlfriend home by curfew. About halfway there, we took a curve too fast. We took out about 200 feet of hog fence, then hit a culvert, and his girlfriend was thrown from the car. We were laying on our sides. It took forever to climb out. We were looking for his girlfriend. I was scared. She was under the car. Thankfully, she wasn't hurt. You've heard of making amends. Well, we made amends to that fence for the next two weekends.

Years later, I was riding with the same friend and another guy who lived in Chicago. He had brought his girlfriend with him. Our friend was driving too fast. I told him to slow down. He couldn't make the curve we were about to hit. His girlfriend curtly turned to the backseat and informed me that I wasn't driving. Me and my buddy took it upon ourselves to brace for what was coming. I laid in the floor and he laid on top of me. We knew the drill by now. During that last wreck, he had been on bottom. Minutes later, the car was on its side, but we climbed out unscathed. The girlfriend's knees were bleeding. I had to ask her as we walked for miles, "Who's driving now?" I couldn't resist.

All us boys started running around together and there was a new game in town, a roller skating rink. We all started learning how to roller skate. Well, this got wild real quick. It wasn't long until we took over the rink. We played tag, tripping each other. The manager was pretty loose with us but when others were skating we had to stay cool. I got tripped one night when I was skating backwards. I hit my head and was knocked out cold. That slowed us down for a little while. Another night in the life of Southern living, learning and growing.

Back in the day, we would just ride around looking for whatever come up. One night we were cruising around and the police spotted us and pulled us over. We were unaware someone had broken into one of the stores the night before. It just so happened a couple of nights earlier, one of my friends had had trouble with someone, and I didn't know he had placed a tire tool from my trunk into the back floor of my car. Well, it didn't take the police but a few minutes to find the tire tool. It fit what the police said was used to pry open the door at the store. So, they took us down to the station to check out our story as to where we were the night of the robbery.

They put us in this room to question us. They left us in there. Well, there we were. We weren't thieves, but we were mischievous and we started to get bored. We spotted these shiny boots sitting under a coat rack, and there was a box of thumbtacks on the desk. If you had known us, you could easily guess the rest. One of the guys put the thumbtacks in the boots.

It was close to shift change. We didn't think of that. In walked this fellow, took off his shoes, reached over and got a pair of the boots. Then, we were sweating. He pulled on his boots and yelled out "I'LL KILL THAT *&#@."

It appeared these guys played jokes on each other just like we did. What a relief that was!

Well, the police checked out our story with the police from our town. See, the local police kept up with us when we were in town. They knew where we were. Again, we did nothing criminal but we were into pranks and laughs and good ole teenage boy mischief.

One of our favorite things to do was play bumper tag. The object of the game was to tag someone's bumper with your bumper and then they were it until they tagged someone else's bumper. These older cars were a lot tougher than today's cars. They had metal bumpers.

Another fun thing we did sometimes was to gather in the street and start pointing up to the sky and exclaiming, "There's one! I just saw it!" UFO's were a topic of conversation back then. Even back in our rural area that sometimes seemed a long way from the rest of the world, we thought about the same things, just maybe in different ways. We never saw anything but we would have half the town claiming they had seen one, too. The reported details varied. Some said what they saw was green, others said it was blue and on and on.

We even had some of the same boys who pranked others afraid to go out in the country to park. Some of the stories were so wild I began to believe them myself. There was nothing like those summer nights.

I would like to mention we parked and listened to WLS Chicago with Dick Biondi, so far away yet so close. By this time, I got myself a 1955 black and white Ford Victoria Hard Top with cruiser skirts, glass packs, that would run 120 MPH. Beautiful car. In the day, this was what was called a panty dropper.

Things were really changing in the 50's. Rock and roll was in the air and everybody wanted to dance. The boys and girls were moving and grooving, dancing. Parents were scared to death of how the kids were acting and rebelling, acting out, etc.

One day while heading to town, I had my youngest brother with me. My radio had to be jarred on sometimes. The road we were traveling was pretty level. I told my brother to watch the road while I leaned over and hit the radio on the bottom. Well, he was watching me instead of the road. Thud! We ran off the road into the field. I came back on the road after a rough maneuver or two. My brother's eyes were wide open now. He said, "I'll watch next time!" We had a big laugh about it since we didn't tear anything up.

Just down the road was a dead end with a drop-off into a hay field and it would feel like you were driving right off the map. Sometimes me and my friends would pick up some girls. Me and the boys would sit in the front seat, the girls in the back just riding and talking. Then all of a sudden, my friend would yell out "Dead end!" I would pretend I was trying to stop. The girls would scream and hit the floor. Then I would be in the hayfield spinning around and around.

The fear in their screams was exhilarating but I'm sure they didn't appreciate our humor very much. After all, a hayfield is very much like ice when it's about five inches tall. I guess the farmer has forgotten about it by now. I hope so. I've always heard the old saying, "it won't make a difference a hundred years from now." I guess that's true about most things but I bet it would be a hundred years from now before those girls would ride with me again.

There was this one girl that stole my heart when I was real young. I was so head-over-heels I couldn't stand it. When you are young, you think it's the world when your heart is broken. Life does go on, but it sure moves mighty slow for a few days.

I wouldn't have worried so much then about girls if I had known I would meet the woman I've been with for fifty years. I did know her most of her life. Occasionally, she would come down to Tennessee for vacation and I would see her. She would stick her tongue out at me and I thought she was a brat. More to come after about my loving wife.

Back to the boyhood mischief I was always apt to be into, especially those Halloween nights. I remember the water balloons and egg throwing, how the police chased us. It was hard for the police to catch us. We scurried like a covey of quails when the police stopped and got out. They never caught us.

As I told you in the beginning, there were bootleggers in town and I was an eager customer. One bootlegger in particular was down by the cotton gin. We had been going over to him to get our liquor, and once when we went back, we were told "Get out! We don't sell liquor!" Well, we were all in a full pickup truck and we were not happy we were being denied service. His house was by the gin and there were lots of empty cotton trailers sitting around. The blacktop was right up against his house. We decided if he wouldn't sell to us, we'd run one of the cotton trailers into his house. I had the tongue of the trailer guiding it while the others were pushing. We had had just enough to drink to be brave. Just as we got about twenty feet away, I was going to drop the tongue and run.

I looked up and the man that had turned us away was standing on the front porch with a shotgun. As I ran through some weeds, I ran right up on a place where a stop sign used to be. The sign was gone, but the pole was not. Just as I ran into the pole, he fired that shotgun. The pole was very flexible. It slammed me down. I got up and ran to the pick-up. They were driving off as I jumped into the back. I looked up and was glad to see that one of the boys, my friend who coincidentally only had one leg, had beaten me to the truck.

After a while, it became very funny, after we were sure no one was hit and we had only ended up with some scratches from the weeds. Never again would I do this. Ha. Ha.

Out in the country on a gravel road was a strawberry patch. One Halloween we took a bunch of crates and stacked them all across the road. Someone went flying down the road and tore up several of the crates. We sat pretty quiet for a while. We laid real low. No one ever knew it was us.

I guess the next prank we pulled was the funniest thing ever. We would take a big brown paper sack (like we used to get at the grocery store) fill it up with fresh cow manure with lots in the bottom, take it and put it on somebody's front porch and set it on fire. Then, we would ring the doorbell and run away, tripping and laughing as we got far enough away to turn and see the victim (sometimes in house shoes and sometimes barefoot) trying to stomp out the fire with cow shit flying everywhere. This was a rib tickler for sure.

Things were so different then. We had manners and we would never talk like kids do today and any of our elders would set us straight if we ever got too "off-colored." For example, there was a country store where teenagers hung out on Saturday nights. It had a big open floor where we stood around playing the juke box and pinball machines. Well, one Saturday night, there were several young folks just hanging out. Most of my friends were there since this was our hangout. The owner had cases of things just sitting around. There were cases in a stack of blue Cheer washing powders. One of my friends sat down on the washing powders and made a statement. "Don't sit here, you will get your underwear blue." Before you could say "skat," the owner came out from behind the counter. He had a 45 mm in his hand and started shouting "Get out, we are not having filthy talk in here!"

As we were lining up to leave, I somehow ended up in the back of the pack. My buddy in front of me said something to me. I told him, "I'm coming back." I wasn't really all that brave. I actually didn't know he was right behind me. He put the barrel into my back and said "What did you say?"

I gulped and said "Nothing." We got outside. Everyone started jawing "He don't scare me" and so on. My buddy looked at me and said, "What's wrong with you?"

I told him about the gun in my back. He said, "You've just become a chicken right in front of my eyes."

That was a serious charge. "Oh yeah? You didn't feel the steel barrel in your back."

I got the gun-wielder back several years later. I was shooting pool with my brother and some other guys. As we played I thought one of the guys looked familiar. No one had called his name. We were taking turns buying beer. Just as it came my turn to buy, I remembered him as the store owner. As I was ordering the beer, I told the server get a beer for everyone except this man.

He said, "You just playing around."

I said "no. I quit school because they had recess. I don't play."

"What did I do?" he continued to ask. So, I brought him up to speed and he said, "I'm sorry that happened. You don't understand. You and the other boys you ran with had a bad name. I was afraid you guys would jump me so I pulled the gun to scare you guys." I laughed it off and let it go.

Another memory I have is about a set of twins who rode my school bus. They both had a crush on me. They looked just alike. I couldn't tell one from the other. Well, both of the girls wanted to sit with me on the bus and who was I to argue? I was always getting into trouble with them. I liked them both. I couldn't tell one from the other. Well, I would play up to one of them and the other would get mad. I didn't know who to try and make up with. This was fun while it lasted. I was always good at getting into trouble with them.

Another memorable girl was this Mexican girl I took on a boat ride so I asked her to go out to an amusement park with me. She agreed. I said, "Where can I pick you up?"

She said, "I will pick you up." I didn't have a car and wasn't old enough to drive anyway so she told me where to be for our "date." I expected her to walk up when I got to the meeting spot, where I figured we would catch a bus. I was looking up and down the street for her and was starting to think she was a no-show. All of a sudden, a limousine pulled up she got out and told me to get in.

Well, I jumped right inside and said with widened eyes, "What's this?"

She told me this was her driver/chaperone. As we got to the park, the driver got out, walked us to the gate, paid for our tickets and gave her some money. He dismissed us with, "Have a good time." Then, he turned to me and said, "Be here at 10:00 PM and don't be late." I didn't know who he was but I knew I wouldn't be late.

I asked her, "What's this all about?"

She said, "You don't need to ask questions, I will be leaving in a few days, going back to Mexico." We enjoyed the night and I stopped with the questions.

I saw her once more and this time I was asking questions. Things like that didn't happen where I lived. It was like something out of a movie. She let me know just before she left that her father was in the mob. What are ya gonna do? That was that. I told you it's easy for me to get into all kinds of mischief.

Not long after my first car, I was in the market for another. This time I found a 1955 Ford Victoria two-door hard top with black and white cruiser skirts, dual exhausts, glass packs, and great sound. This was a girl magnet. I was very lucky to have a car, not that many guys had cars in the 50's. The ones that were lucky enough to have had a car had lots of friends. The very day my best friend and I bought this car we were on the way home and laughing and talking, really excited. Well a car pulled out right in front of us and we went all over the road before landing in a small ditch with dust flying. We got everything under control and looked over the car to surprisingly find there wasn't a scratch on it. They don't make them that tough anymore.

Things were changing fast in the South, with our boy Elvis being labeled as the greatest thing since sliced bread. Teenagers were being rebels, we listened to Chicago WLS, Bick B on our car radios. Rock and roll was everything, along with white shoes, poodle skirts, and pony tails. The country kids were coming to town cafes, where teens hung out to dance to the tunes on the juke box.

It was very common to be married very young. I didn't get a wife but I did get a real job. Me and my friend L.R. started working in a garment factory. Well, you know, it was mostly all women and, oh, we were in the clover field. I made myself a promise before starting to write that I wouldn't talk about some topics and this would be one of them, but let's say we didn't have any problems finding dates with a hot car. No problems at all. L.R. and I would go on double dates. We would take the girls to our old standby, the drive-in theater, or maybe just cruising up and down the main drag. It was mostly just innocent fun.

None of us had money so we were all in the same boat. We lived close to Reelfoot Lake. This provided lots of fun days. On the lake there was swimming and fishing. One of our hangouts was The Roundhouse. It was just a covered pavilion, but there was a concession stand with a juke box. Saturdays and Sundays were really crowded. It seemed like every kid in town was there. The dance floor was concrete and mostly girls danced with other girls. The boys were shy or didn't know how to dance. Many times we would get car loads and spend the day at the Roundhouse.

Where we lived there were several young girls and guys within three or four miles of each other. Everybody knew each other. My car was pretty fast and I drove pretty fast most of the time. Once, while we were riding around we went to the Roundhouse where some of the girls from our neighborhood asked if they stayed and danced, could we let them ride home with us. We agreed.

One of the girls with us was a girl I had been dating from time to time. On the way home I guess I was driving a little too fast and some of the roads toward home were gravel. Well, we did what we called "fish tailing" on the gravel. These girls were hanging on for dear life. When we got to the store close to where everyone lived, one of the girls got out and kissed the pavement and said, "You will never have to worry about giving me another ride!" I guess driving has always been in my blood, even if it wasn't always appreciated. Well, I guess she told her mother, so then I had to beg the mother to let her daughter ride with me after that. And I did. I really loved this girl's mother and respected her so when she allowed her to date me, I promised to drive safely and I did.

One time, we were following a car on a narrow road and the driver was going very slow and was driving in the middle of the road. After a few minutes, someone said, "Push him." Well, wild and young kicked in, so I pulled up to this guy's bumper and pushed him up to maybe 50 MPH.

When I finally backed off his bumper, he pulled over and let us go by. We had lots of good times in that car. We didn't have much money, but we always had fun. Life was so simple back then, just living our young lives in the South. Several of our friends would get together on a sand bar, park and open the doors, turn the radio as loud as she would go, and build a huge driftwood fire. We would roast hot dogs and have a tub iced down with our drinks. We danced, told jokes, laughed and had a great time, and we didn't bother anyone. Very few of the adults even knew we did this on Saturday nights.

We always cruised around on Sunday afternoons. The town was usually quiet. Mostly, we teenagers pretty much had the town to ourselves. The police watched but didn't bother us unless we got really out of hand. I remember this one Sunday, I was stopped in the street talking to someone going the other way. We had the street blocked. A car pulled up behind me and after a couple of minutes, instead of blowing his horn, he got out and walked up to my door. He was an older fellow, huge compared to my little skinny ass. I won't mention his name.

He says to me, "Do you have a church key?"

A church key was what we called what was used as a can opener. I said "Sure."

He had a can of beer in his hand. You couldn't buy beer on Sunday back then so I could tell he was pretty serious about his beer. This wasn't a boy. This was a man. I handed him my can opener.

He tapped on the can a couple times and opened the can and handed me my church key and also the can of beer. What was I going to do? I took it and drank a big swallow.

Meanwhile, all of this is going on in the middle of town in the street. I was still kind of sweating because I didn't know what he was going to do. He looked me dead in the eye and said "Boy, that just kept you from getting an ass whooping." I was out of his way before he got back to his car. Oh yes, he would have done it. He must have been in a good mood. Otherwise, I might have been bruised up a bit.

Just like in Rebel Without a Cause and Grease, one of our big things was drag racing. My little Ford was not the fastest thing around but she held her own. She would run the hand off the numbers. This was one of the toughest cars I believe Ford ever made. Chevy was coming out with the big blocks with the '57 and '58 Chevies. Those were bad-to-the-bone back then. One guy I knew had a '57 Chevy convertible and as far as I know, it was never beat. You would think it was real heavy being a convertible, but he made that car fly.

His brother was my best friend. Sometimes he let us use his car. His brother would tell us, "Don't drag race my car. If you do and get beat, I'll beat you!" My friend would take a chance every once in a while, when he knew we couldn't get beat unless he missed a gear or something. I was always afraid for him because he wasn't as good of a driver as his brother. This was one hot Chevy.

Well, my best friend met this older girl who had her own car. These two were like glue. Me and my friend didn't get to see each other like we used to. She took up most of his time. We had dated lots of the same girls, one of whom I thought was the one he would marry, but that wasn't to be. Soon, my best friend was married to someone else. Something I'm not proud of today is that I had lost the girl I thought was mine. Sometimes we don't know what's in store for us. There's a song that says I thank God for unanswered prayers. Well, that's true.

We had such a good group of friends and the things we thought would happen for each other or ourselves didn't always come to fruition, but it all worked out just like it was supposed to.

When I first started my real job in a garment factory, I was a bundle boy. This is someone who gets the materials to the sewing operators. Well, after a while, the owners liked me so they put me in training to be a sewing machine mechanic. All these machine operators were women, and most were young women. This was like a buffet bar and all the males were hungry.

These women were always needing something done to their machines, so I was in popular demand. My boss wanted me to go to school in New York for repairing the sewing machines, but I had no interest in doing that. Some of the girls who were machine operators were girls I had once tried to date, but now they were married and suddenly wanted to go out. We will leave that right there.

This was a sign of the times, the women taking jobs outside the home. Before, women took care of the house, including the care of their husbands and kids. They suddenly weren't staying in the kitchen anymore. The South was waking up. As we were growing up, boys and girls were looking for new things.

We were still usually in town every night doing something, even if it was just hanging around. One night, we were sitting around watching a pool game. One of our friends came in and said, "Lets ride around." He was in his dad's car so me and two others went riding with him. One of my friends was younger than me. He got in the backseat. All of a sudden, the driver pulled over in front of a grocery store, one of the guys with us jumped out and grabbed a case of bananas. We rode out into the country, opened the case up, and found out all of them were green.

I was always up for mischief, but never one for just out and out breaking the law, so I talked them into taking the bananas back to the store. We came back into town to meet up with some friends. They told us the police were looking for us. The police had seen what we had done. Me and my friends got out and started walking home. We lived about eight miles out of town. It was late, so there was no traffic. When I saw headlights coming behind us as we got out of town, I told my friend, "Uh-oh, it's the police."

They slowly pulled along beside us and stopped. They said, "Get in, boys."

I tried to play dumb and said, "What's the problem?"

The officer said he knew about the bananas. I told him I didn't know what he was talking about. I had not looked into the car. About that time, a voice from the backseat says, "Doug, I already told him everything."

I had a little pull with that particular officer and insisted the other boy had nothing to do with it. I agreed to get in if he would let my friend go. It worked. We headed to city hall. One of the boys, one we would call a city slicker, got to go home. His dad was a big shot in town. Sometimes in our rural area it really did matter who you knew. The other dummy was already in jail. The next morning, they moved us to the county jail. As it turned out, they believed me that I didn't know they planned to take the bananas. But they wanted the other boy for a car theft in Chicago and we had to stay in the county jail until his trial came up for car theft across state lines. Small town wheels turn slow.

While we were there, some crazy dude tried to kill us. He was in for 11/29, eleven months and twenty-nine days, and he had been in before, so they let him make leather goods: belts, billfolds, etc. He was a pretty smart guy, even if he was crazy. This fellow had a long string. He would have someone get him a fifth of wine and he would let down the string so the person could attach the bottle to the string. When he got the booze, he would lower his wallet down so payment could be taken out. We were all on the second or third floor.

Well, the man got drunk and he had lots of tools in his cell because he made the billfolds. We were sitting around playing cards when he stormed into our cell and hit this black man in the back with a long steel bar. He tried to hit us, but we got on each side of him and managed to elude him. When he came after one of us, the other came after him. This was winter time and bitterly cold, but he knocked all the windows out before the officers got up there. We almost froze to death. We had no covers.

Later, they lined us all up and questioned us as to what happened. They put this crazy man in the cell by himself. He cursed us all night long. As we were freezing, he would've gotten hurt if we could've gotten to him. The things we heard that man say that night! Shameful.

Well, I had to sit it out and do my time until the other guy came to trial. Then, they let me go. For a guy who didn't do anything except go for a ride, I sure went through a lot. One thing I found out is you can't fight city hall.

Chapter 5

The debacle with the bananas was really and truly not my fault, but I learned my lesson. I should have never gotten into that car. After this happened, I went to stay with Brownie in Detroit, Michigan for a fresh start. I must have looked older than I was. My brother had me go get him a six pack of beer from down at the corner store. Nobody ever asked my age. My brother had a brother-in-law named Arthur about my age. One day after I had picked up my brother's beer, I walked with it tucked under my arm. I met up with Arthur and some other boys. As we were walking and talking, he got behind me and knocked the beer from under my arm. The other boys grabbed it and ran. Well, I ran after them. We ended up in a backyard with an old car on blocks and a wheel off of it. They were already popping the tops and drinking my beer. Not long after I caught up with them, we heard the sirens nearby. We didn't think much about it until they stopped at this house. The yard had a fence around it. I climbed the fence. I was on top of the fence. The cops shouted, "Stop or I'll shoot!"

I was so skinny I could stand in the shade of a clothes line. I was what you might call straddled over the fence. I fell back into the yard. They took all of us in. Guess what? They let everybody go but me. Those cops must have wanted to set an example of me, being an outsider from the South and all. They charged me with contributing to underage youth. I was underage myself. They put me on probation for one year.

Brownie picked me up. I didn't get into trouble. It seemed my brother had somewhat of a reputation himself. Even though he was married, he would still run with his buddies on the weekends. He had a beautiful '53 Chevy Bel-Air convertible, red and white. He let me drive it. I don't guess he cared whether I had a license or not. We would bar hop and shoot pool. He was pretty good with a cue stick. We would go in and he would always place his money on the table to play whoever won. Then he would do all the betting. One time we had the table for hours. We had won some money. We were playing 8 ball.

Brownie was really good if we just drank some beer but he would get a little wild on liquor. I made the 8 ball without calling my shot and we lost. It made him so mad. Up north, people called you names and he thought nothing of it, but he never got to the point where he was accepting of someone calling him a son-of-a-bitch. If he knew you really well, he would say, "Smile when you say that." If he didn't know you, well, he would throw something. He never planned on fighting fair, just fighting enough to get through another day.

One night, one of his real good friends was home from the armed services and several of us were sitting around a big table. The club was out from town a little ways. There was a sailor and a soldier working to get some young ladies to dance. (My brother always wore a sport jacket, no tie). Well, these two boys got to arguing. My brother said, "Joe can't fight you. He is not supposed to be here."

Well, this big guy got up and said, "My friend can't fight either." Guys in the armed services were not supposed to be involved in bar brawls or other acts that did not reflect positively on our fine military.

My brother said, "Well you don't want to mess up your nice coat. Take it off."

I'm saying, "Oh, no, let's get out of here," and all the while, this guy was taking off his coat. You have seen this movie before.

While this guy was taking off the coat, just as both arms were tied up, Brownie let him have it. Down he went. Everybody was fighting. I was underage as well as on probation, so I crawled out from underneath everybody. I got the car and let the top down just as they were running out. They jumped in the car, all the while, screaming, Go! Go! Go!"

It wasn't long before we heard sirens. The cops were on their way but still there was no sign of my brother. The guys were still yelling at me to go, but I wasn't leaving without my brother. All of a sudden, out came my brother and jumped into the car. I took off. We got going, and met the cops. To our great fortune, they didn't even look at us. They were trying to get to the club. It was a nice feeling that I had gotten away with something after that last episode with the bananas.

For a time, Brownie's older brother-in-law, Grover, did sand blasting. Where they worked, they got in several jobs for the winter months and they needed someone to sand pot for them while they sand blasted. All they asked me was whether or not I had a social security card. I told them I did and I was hired. Here's a little FYI about sandblasting: you don't want to get blasted.

The armor was made of a heavy, canvas-type material. You had to use several PSI's to really blast. We would go inside rail cars and use jack hammers to knock off the build-up of chemicals that had been in the cars. We had to wear air masks to breathe. Sometimes we would still get high by accident. After the thick layers were hammered off, we would blast with sand to get back to the metal. The only way you could get in and out of these tanker cars was through a hole in the top.

When I went in, I always took the largest air hose I could find to take with me. I had a fear of getting closed up. These guys were always playing jokes. I tried not to give them a chance to close me up. While all of this was going on, the chemical plant had no place to store the acid they were making. So, we started building pits to store the acid in 100,000 gallon pits. We built them ten feet apart. Upon finishing, we would get inside them and make sure no rocks or anything were in there to cause a leak in the liner we were putting in. This was during the cold winter in Detroit Michigan. No matter the snow, ice, cold, you still worked.

The acid was strong. We were putting it into the pits. When the wind was blowing the right direction, the acid would put holes in the stocking of the ladies who crossed the parking lot to get to their offices. When the wind was really blowing, you had to stand with the pits in front of you. One day I was pushing a wheel barrow between the pits. A supervisor came over and asked, "Do you have gold teeth?"

I said, "No. Why?"

He said, "If you fall in there, that's the only way we could know who you are." As I said earlier, I was as skinny as a rail, but I had made friends with this one really big man. I think he was an Indian. He took care of me. He took the heavy load off of me and didn't let anyone pick on me.

The boss told us we had one hundred thousand dollars' worth of life insurance on us. It would be double in the event of an accident. I thought for a short moment that if I fell in, my mom would be rich. This was a lot of money back then, but I got over that thought quick.

Later in the spring I went to see my probation officer. The guy I had been working with was going to Alabama, so I told my probation officer I was going back to Tennessee. He said, "You can't leave the state."

I told him, "You hide and watch me."

He talked about putting me in lock up. I wasn't worried because these had all been drummed up charges anyway. So, I said goodbye to Detroit, and caught a ride to Nashville with the guys that were going to Alabama. Then I got me a bus ticket in Nashville to head back home. Well, I looked over my shoulder for months because of the threats of the probation officer, but no one ever came for me. I did go back to Michigan some years later but not for a long while.

I got back home in April. Trees were starting to get green. Life was good. I didn't have a real job, just getting along, living the carefree life. What came or went made no difference. I started drinking and messing where I shouldn't be messing. I was at a bad point in life. I had a sawed-off shot gun under my seat and a handgun in my waist belt. I think I pushed things as far as I could have and further than I should have. I had some close calls.

One time I was lit up and the woman I was with took my gun and unloaded it and gave it back to me. When I got back to myself, I looked at my gun. It was empty. It started me to thinking that I had to change the way I was living. Around this time, I decided to see a movie. I ran into a friend of mine. He knew I had a gun. Some man was after him. Not just any man, a mean man. He wanted my gun.

I told him, "It's under my front seat, loaded." This was a good a way as any to start with a clean slate. I told him to keep it, forget where he got it and never tell anyone it came from me. A sawed-off shotgun was a federal offense. I think it carried a ten-year term. The next day I dumped the handgun and parked my car in my parents' front yard and that was that.

The Fourth of July that year, hot and sticky as it always was in Tennessee in late summer, found me at the beautiful Reelfoot Lake. I ran into Tommy, a good friend of mine, at the who told me he was going to Chicago to stay with his uncle. By this time, I had decided I was headed up to the windy city as well. We talked about getting together once when we got there. We both had family working for the same company and had heard it was easy to get a job there if they liked your family members.

I headed to Chicago where I stayed with my sister and her family. My brother-in-law was employed by this company, so I went to work there and I was working on an assembly line where they made pinball machines and shuffle alleys, juke boxes and other things, including two-way radios for the government. This was my reset. I was starting life over, turning over a new leaf (as they say), and leaving my old life behind. This was to be the first day of the rest of my life.

I met up with Tommy, who was staying with his uncle. His uncle was from the South also. I knew them from my friend's family. When I went to see my friend at his uncle's house, I had no idea I would someday be married to his daughter. Almost every day we walked all around the neighborhood looking at used car lots. Sometimes his cousin would go with us. We went to Riverview Amusement Park. At the time, they had the fastest roller coaster anywhere. It was The Fireball. Riverview was where everyone went. They had everything you could think of.

After we had been working for a while, I started buying cheap old cars and cleaning them up, washing and waxing them to resell or trade them. Once, I bought an old car and traded it to my friend for a hat. You couldn't use a hat as currency on Ebay today, but it worked back then.

My sister Ludine and her husband Boots lived in an apartment building and I made friends with most of the young folks around. Most of the families had migrated from the South for better job opportunities. When I was young, I was always getting a sore throat. One of these guys that lived in the building was from Alabama. He had been on vacation and had brought back some moonshine. He told me, "Here, drink some of this, it'll go away." I took some and gargled. I didn't drink it. The next morning I coughed and spit some crap out of my throat. It didn't hurt again for years.

This guy had also bought one of the old Chicago police three-wheel motorcycles. I don't know if it had plates or not but for sure I didn't have a driver's license. He allowed me to ride the thing all the time. My friend and my future wife would come over. She always wanted to ride the motorcycle with me. My wife is younger than me. I should have known better than to ride without a license, but we never got caught or hurt. Thank God. We had the most fun riding all over the north side of Chicago. We lived close to Lincoln Park.

One friend I worked with had a boat. On his boat, Don would cruise just outside of the barrier for boats and the beach. We would just idle along until we saw girls sunbathing. All we had to do was wave and they would be right out there, wanting to sunbathe on his boat. We would take them for rides out into Lake Michigan while they sunbathed. Neither the lake nor the girls were bad to look at. Don was a German, a real friendly kind of guy, and we spent lots of time on the boat. One day, we were going out in the boat and I wanted to ski. We went by my future in-laws' house and I talked him into going with us. He had never ever gone with us before and he never went again, but this one time he saved my life. Of that I'm sure.

We got out on the lake and Don was having trouble keeping the motor running. Like I said, it was Chicago. They don't call Chicago the windy city for nothing. Well, I was out in the water. Waves were really high and I lost my life preserver. Instead of trying to pick it up, I started swimming for the boat and the motor had died. It was drifting away from me. I couldn't swim as fast as the wind was taking the boat from me.

I began to give out. Well as luck would have it, Don got the motor started. Guess what? He went further away from me in order to circle me and pick me up. Well, as he started the circle the motor died again. Then, he was further away. I started to panic, but I told myself to stay calm and tread water for a few minutes. I did, but the boat was drifting ever further away. So, I started to swim toward the boat again. I was totally given out. Don cranked the motor again and he circled me all this time.

My future father-in-law was watching me. He was aware I was in trouble but Don was working on the motor and lost track of time on my situation this time. As he went by me, (and in my mind, I call him my Savior at that moment), he threw a lifeline to me. I put it over my head and my arms through it and just like that they popped me right up into the boat. As I climbed over the side of the rail, I blacked out for a couple of seconds. That's how close I came to not being able to write about it.

Soon, Don got him a '65 Mustang, two plus two, 289 high performance four-speed. It was hot. We had some good races in that thing. Mundelein, Illinois, right off Interstate 94, had a nudist colony. We took lots of rides up that way. The owner of the company where I worked was Chicago connected, if you know what I mean. He had a penthouse above the plant. He parked on one end of the building and walked through a covered walk all the way to the other side of the building where his penthouse was located. It was like Fort Knox to get to him.

I had the pleasure of cleaning up some times when he wasn't there. Inside, he had a full bar, shoe shine stand, pool table, jukebox, and pinball machines (which we made there). This was something this country boy had not seen anything like in his life. He was very private and we never heard anything about him.

Across the street was a little café that served breakfast and lunch only. My brother-in-law always ate breakfast there. This is where I got my first taste of French toast. The owner and cook was the best old lady and she didn't cook anything that wasn't good. When I first got up there in Chicago, I didn't have much money. I rode to work with my brother-in-law. As I said, we always ate breakfast at the little cafe. When I asked him for anything he always told me, "I'm not putting out nothing but eyeballs," and he would shake his fist at me. Nevertheless, he would give me whatever help he could. I thought of him as a brother.

I really was close to him. He had a house full of kids to feed. Once, where we lived was close to the Chicago housing projects. You know the show Good Times? They lived in the projects. Remember they were always saying, "The cops won't even come here"? There were gangs all over the projects. A couple of brothers from down South lived across from me. One of them had surgery. He had to walk so much every day. One day as we walked by the projects, some guys came after us. They threw their bottles and things but didn't hit either of us. Then they tried to block the sidewalk. One of the brothers had a switchblade knife. He gave it to his brother. As we came closer to them, he popped it open. He said, "Cut 'em."

We were lucky. The cops pulled up from all over the place. We just kept walking. The police didn't bother us. They just busted up the gang. There were those tense moments from time to time, but it wasn't always bad in the city. I can remember when I worked at Lincoln Park. It was great to be among the many people walking around, the kids would be laughing, hollering, and having fun just enjoying themselves. Again, I have to say life was so simple back then.

I played baseball on a church league back then. We had several teams. Our church required you go at least twice monthly in order to play. There were some really good teams. I pitched and was first baseman and catcher. Once when I was playing my best ever, the second baseman let one get through by him and the coach pulled me. I was not happy.

I remember once when we were playing baseball, I was playing first base and this was kite weather in Chicago. During the spring, everybody flies kites. There would be all kinds of colors and shapes. Well, I was watching a kite flying high in the air while the guy up to bat was a no-hitter who was really bad. But on this day, as luck would have it, he hit a line drive right at me as I turned, I threw my hand up to keep the ball from hitting me in the face. I ended up with a broken little finger. It's still crooked to this day. I put popsicle sticks on each side and taped it but it didn't work. By night time, it was hurting extremely bad. I removed the sticks. I learned my lesson: don't take your eye off the ball.

We would participate in pool tournaments in the winter time. When you lost, you were out, and that was it but we would always hang around and watch the games to see who won. There were some really good players.

Chicago summers featured beautifully landscaped parks and we spent time at the parks and the beach. The laid-out flower beds were always beautiful in the spring and summer. At the beach, we would be fishing, swimming, and laying out down by the lake. There were lots of young people who would take their cars and wax them. We would spend all day playing music and cleaning cars, drinking beer and just chilling out all day.

The sailboats were so beautiful, all the white sails against the blue-green lake water. It was really something to see. The weather was very pleasant on the lake, with cool breezes to counter the hot summers. Young couples would park all along the lakefront. If you didn't get there early, you didn't get a parking space. Chicago was like all cities, I guess. You have the low rent districts and the very rich neighborhoods. Chicago is such a diverse place. Just like big cities have Chinatown, where folks of that ethnicity sometimes go to enjoy a meal and enjoy a taste of home, we had our Southern sections in Chicago. Some of these areas where the Southern people came to eat were nice and some were dirty. It seemed there were places for people from all nations and different backgrounds.

There is something for everyone in a city like Chicago. I worked with some ladies from Poland and Germany. They were so funny. They would give me advice. They would tell me "Jimbo, when you first get married it's 'honey, honey' for the first year, then it's 'hey, you.'" They were very competitive with one another and both wanted to be in the center of everything.

Our accountant was also a jokester. He had two beautiful daughters. I asked him, "Casey, how in the world did you come up with such beautiful girls?"

He said, "I didn't make them with my face, but you should see their mother. She is pretty all over." He could be a dirty old man.

Christmas time rolled around. The owner always gave us a party. I was elected the bartender each time we had a party. The owner got the liquor. He always included a fifth of Southern Comfort. He told me this was my private stock. I really didn't like whiskey, but he didn't know that. I guess he figured I drank whiskey because I was from the South. That would be my drink. I would mix up drinks for my special ladies from down South with Southern Comfort.

A really good friend of mine was the plant manager's secretary. We did a lot of work together. I really treasured our friendship. When I was to move back to Tennessee, she cried for a week. It was years before I realized she was in love with me. I didn't look at it that way. We were such good friends. She was as close to me as a sister, but I guess she saw it differently.

After I moved back home in the South, I would always go back and visit the plant and all my friends. She finally told me years after I had moved to Tennessee that she loved me. I can genuinely say I was floored. I was so in love with my wife and nobody was thought of that way by me. Everybody else said they saw it, but not me. They say love is blind. That's true because I couldn't see anything except the woman who was my wife.

There were adventures at work as well. One day at work, one of the ladies came running up to me. "You must come quickly! They need your help!" As I started down on the floor, an 18-year-old female came running through the building just like the day she was born except now she's all female, if you know what I mean. She was as naked as a jaybird and had three big guys chasing her. They had already tackled her in the maintenance department and they had oil all over them. She had managed to break free from all three of them after they had gotten her down before she had managed to break away and run through the plant. Now this wasn't a case of someone eluding an attack as it may sound. No, this was a young girl who seemed to be having some kind of crazy, psychotic fit and the men were trying to stop her and cover her up.

One of the ladies put a sheet around her. I had a 64 Chevy convertible 409 four speed. I let the top down. We tried to get her through the door of the building, but she seemed to be in shock or something. She would put her feet against the door facing and we couldn't get her through. Finally, we managed to get her outside. I threw her in the back seat, but she was still hysterical and the floor lady who had been helping jumped in on top of her and tried to hold her down. I took off for the nearest hospital. We were on a four-lane street part of the time.

Although Helen, the floor lady, tried her best to keep her covered up, her hysteria caused her to fight Helen's help and the truckers were getting an eyeful. Cars were blowing their horns. People were hollering. The girl peed all in my seat. As we got to the hospital, I went in on a one-way lane the wrong way. A cop saw me and started to flag me down. As soon as he saw what was happening, he waved me on.

They had a wheelchair waiting at the entrance. We got the scared girl out of the car. She overtook Helen. A helpful large man helped me to put her in the wheelchair. As we got into the hospital, she started choking the life out of me. I was trying to tell the doctor to get her off me. The doctor just kept on trying to get a needle in her arm. Well, it took my best left hook I had to knock her loose. After several minutes of fighting with her, the doctor finally got enough meds in her to calm her down.

We found out at the hospital this hadn't been the girl's first rodeo. Once before, she had stripped off her clothes and had threatened to jump out a window. Later, Helen and I were questioned about how the girl got a black eye and bruises. She told police I had blacked her eye. I said, "Officer I was driving, how could I have done that?" Our company ended up using a company lawyer to get us cleared of charges.

This is one of those times where you would have to be there. I'm telling you she was all woman. You can figure out the rest.

There was another time we had this young Puerto Rican girl cut her hand on one of the presses. I took her to the hospital. They kept her overnight. The next day my boss came back to my office and told me to go pick her up from the hospital and take her home. Somebody had brought her an overnight bag but no one could take her home. My boss instructed me not to let her lift anything and make sure she got inside her house before I left her. Got it.

I drove her home and I was carrying her bag and all. Well, she unlocked the door and told me to put my bag over on the bed. That would mean I would have to come into the house. I put the bag by the door. She grabbed me and tried to pull me inside. "Come on in," she demanded. I don't know who else was there, if anyone, but I got the heck out of there.

Then my boss's bookkeeper wanted me to take her bar hopping down in Hillbilly Heaven, as we called it. She just wanted to see what went on in that section of the city. Well, at least every other night someone would get thrown through the front glass window in this part of town. I stayed away from these joints, but I finally agreed to take her. After about the second bar we went into, I figured out that this was not her first rodeo. We ordered a beer. The bar was pretty dark. I noticed she didn't look around to see where the bathrooms were, but she got up, and walked straight to the bathroom. She came back. I said, "Let's go."

She said, "Why do you want to leave?"

I replied, "Because, Sister, you lied to me about not being here before."

She denied it at first but when I confronted her about knowing where the bathrooms were, she admitted she had been there before. She told me she had just wanted to get me to come out with her.

I didn't do this anymore. Another time, me and my buddy, the one with the boat and Mustang, were out on the town. We went to a strip club. Our dancer was in front of us on the bar. Don wasn't feeling any pain. She squatted down in front of him and pulled his head between her legs. He pulled back like he was going to hit her. By that time, four Big Boys walked us out of the door.

We weren't done for the night and went into another strip club. The dancer was wearing something that looked like pantyhose. It was cold, really cold, that night and we had been walking for a while before we went in. This girl backed up her butt in front of me and Don. He didn't think about what he was doing. He took his cold coins out of his pocket, pulled the garment open and it filled it up with cold coins. You guessed it. She screamed and we were out of there.

One time Don called me at two in the morning to come bail him out. He had been picked up for driving under the influence. I got down to the station to bail him out and one of the roughest, quick-to-brawl boys that ever came out of Tennessee was being booked for something or another. My guess was that he was facing charges for fighting or maiming someone. He was telling the police if they would take off their guns and badges he would beat the crap out of them. The cops were goading him, asking, "Do you think you can?"

About that time the guy spotted me. He came and put his arm around me and told the cops, "This old boy here picked cotton with me. You touch him, you got me to fight."

They booked him and another man and the desk clerk said, "He was nuts to think he could whip all three of us."

What do you think I said? All I know is the last fight I saw him in was in a bar. He took on four other tough, good ole Southern boys and then it took several cops to beat him down with nightsticks to load him in the paddy wagon. I finally got Don out, took him home and had to take him back the next day to get his car. Now we both were dead. We had to answer to Don's Dad about why we were both late. I don't remember his excuse. I dreamed up something.

Mr. Weiss was the German owner of the plastics plant where I worked. He was also one of the best men I knew. He was also stern, but fair. Once, the plant manager got onto me out in the plant, so I walked out and the owner's son walked with me. We went fishing for about three days. We came back on a Friday.

Don went in to get his check and his dad said, "Where's Jim?"

He told him I was in the car, waiting on him. He sent him out to get me. I really respected Mr. Weiss, so I agreed to go in to see him. I went in. He told me to sit down. "I want to talk to you."

I did as he said and he continued, "What is so wrong that you walked out?"

I told him I would rather not say. The plant manager was from near where I was from. "Jim it's not like you to walk out. I want to know what happened and I want you back at work tomorrow."

We worked five and a half days every week. I finally told Mr. Weiss what had happened so he called the plant manager into his office. Mr. Weiss told him to figure out how we could settle our differences because I would be back at work tomorrow. I don't think we had another problem. In fact, after I moved back, we stayed in touch with each other for years.

He always wanted me to come down and go fishing with him. Later, he passed on. His wife continued to write to us. She often told me how much her husband thought of my family.

We had three shifts and mostly all women ran the presses. I was there before the 3rd shift went home from work throughout the first shift and was still there when the second shift started. So, I knew all the people on all the shifts. One day I was talking to one of the ladies on second shift. The second shift leader came over and told me not to talk to his women. The shift leader was all jealous of me because I was pretty much my own boss at shipping and receiving, and stocking but I also looked after the owner's car and whatever else he needed me to do. You name it, I did it.

Well, I told Marty, the foreman, I could speak to who I pleased. So, he came by and said, "That son-of-a-b**** won't leave my operators alone."

I said, "What did you say?"

He said, "You heard me."

I warned him to take it back and apologize, but no, he wouldn't do it. So, I told him I would be back that night at midnight to settle it. I went home with the intention of going back when he got off work, but I fell asleep. I woke up around 2 a.m., knowing he had already gone home by then.

I was so mad at myself and the next day I said, "I'll get him when he comes to work. I'll get him outside before he gets in the building." He always parked out back and came down the alley. I watched for him. He always brought his lunch in a large black metal lunch box. I made it into the alley. I have been stewing all night and all day by then. I was really hot and frustrated.

I gave him another chance to take back what he said and he refused. He started, "You are still ---?

That's when I hit him and knocked him down. I'll never forget it. As he was going down, he threw his lunch box in the air and it came down and flew open. There was an apple in it. I looked and saw the apple rolling down the alley and I was watching it just roll and roll. He started to get up, so I got on him and just as he was trying to hit me where it hurts, I punched him again and that was that. He asked me to let him go, so I did.

For several days, he came to work with a long wrench but he never offered to hit me with it. Someone told on me for hitting him. My nemesis was a German fellow and the company owner was German. I told my boss the truth about the whole thing as to what happened. I still had to talk with the machine operators to see if they needed any material or anything, but he never bothered me again.

The plant manager wanted me to know everything about the company as he was planning on retiring. I believe he wanted me to take his place as plant manager. As I was being trained by whoever for whatever job, one man from back home, close to where I was from, told me he wouldn't tell me everything because then I would know what he knew and that was his job. He was so funny. I didn't want his job for nothing. He walked around the machine all the time. It was hot. The cylinders had to reach 400 to 800 degrees. I was perfectly happy in my role as jack-of-all-trades and master of none.

Chapter 6

One winter it snowed really big time. It started one morning and snowed all day and all night. The next morning there was like 30 something inches of snow. The city was at a standstill. I made a mistake. I got my car out of the snow bank and got to work by following an ambulance. There was no place to put the snow. They had every piece of equipment the city owned out moving snow. They dumped it into Lake Michigan. They would fill up coal cans and ship them south until the snow melted before they got to where they were going. As we were digging out, a truck with a big dozer pulled up and unloaded and started pushing the snow away from our loading docks.

We thought the boss hired the guy. Well, he worked for about an hour. At that point, a guy pulled up in a pickup with flashing lights. The driver of the pickup jumped out hollering and cursing, "You are at the wrong address, you dummy!" We got a big laugh out of it, but it sure helped us out. we were busting ice 10 - 20 in thick. This was the most snow I seen at once in my life and I hope I never see this much snow in my life again! I did make a little money from it though. We had a walk-behind little tractor snow plow. I put chains on it to pull out the cars that could not get going. I had a short chain I would hook onto the stuck cars and my little tractor was out in the street with ruts. I would be on pavement. I pulled them out, one after another, and they would pay me whatever they wanted to. This was the 60's so $5 was good money for five minutes.

One day while I was outside, a man decided to come along and run into a parked car. I was watching him so he got out paper and pen and was writing a note. He said, "I'm leaving my information so they can call me to get their car repaired." He put the note on the windshield and left a hurry, so I went over to check it out. His note read, "This man is watching me. He thinks I'm leaving information so you can call me. Sorry about your car." How many people would believe this? Since then I believe half I see and nothing I hear.

This company I worked for was filled with the very best people. It was home to me. I was happy working for them. There was a little store on the corner from the plant that sold sandwiches. We got our lunch there every day. It was German-owned. They made a meatloaf that was sliced, nothing like our Southern meatloaf but it was really good. Leaving from the South and going to a city like Chicago is mind-blowing in every aspect. There were all these foods I had never heard of. I really loved the kosher corned beef with mustard. The Italians had their Chicago Dogs and the list went on and on. When I moved to Chicago I was 29 in the waist. When I left, I was wearing a 30 in the waist because I was always walking. I was working my full-time job and two part-time jobs on the side, so I was always active.

My full-time job was at a place where I molded telephone handles. They had to be buffed so I worked part-time for Jim. I built the buffing machine to buff the handles. I also worked part-time at a hot stamping company. My full-time job was with molded plastics for Bell & Howell (same place)? We hot stamped the numbers on these parts. I learned a lot about how to get it just right to do the stamping. The stamp just had to kiss the products to stay on. I had five or six people working there with me. I had some young ladies doing stamping. A couple of them were pretty wild. One night one of these girls reached out and grabbed one of the young boys that helped stock parts. He told me, "James, James you've got to stop her!" I laughed so hard I had to go to the bathroom so he couldn't see me. One night she asked for a ride to a bar on our way home.

I said, "Sure." As we were on the way over, she reached under her blouse and took off her bra. I asked her what she was doing.

She said nonchalantly, "I'm taking my bra off. I can't go in there with it on." Now, I didn't know it was that easy to get a bra off; it was never that easy for me to get them off. (Just kidding. My wife will read this book. I must be careful as to what I say.)

Speaking of my wife, Lynnette, my life changed for the better when I started spending time with her and her family. I was a different person after being around my future in-laws and my peers at work, like they made joy come out of me. Me and Lynette would go to the movies and visit with our friends at their homes. We would hang out with friends at homes all the time and there were no more wild times with the drinking and laying out.

I started calling my wife Lynn even though her family called her Nette. However, after years with her family, the name Lynn stuck but never with her mom and dad, who were like my own parents. I loved them both very much. Since Lynn was so much younger than me, I understood their concern for their little girl but one thing I know for sure. I've learned after over 50 years of marriage, when Lynn makes up her mind to something, that's it. Lynn said when she and her dad came over to where I lived with my sister, she told me she had said, "That's the one for me."

I didn't think of her that way because of our age difference and other circumstances. As I got to know her, I realized even though she was young, she was very smart, not to mention, very cute. As we went places together with her parents, we started going to the movies and bowling. By this time, I had gotten a car so we would go to Lake Michigan and cruise around, sometimes all the way up to Wisconsin to a Dog & Suds, our favorite place to go up there.

We, as a family, went to Milwaukee to see the Milwaukee Braves play. Once, I was sitting by Pop, Lynn's dad, and the peanut guys came around. My future brother-in-law had one of his girlfriends there and they eventually got peanuts. Pop looks at me while motioning to the girl and said, "Hey, check this out." I looked over and my future brother-in-law's date was eating the shells. All Papa said was, "You need to get her something to eat. She's hungry." He was so funny.

Once, we were in a nice restaurant and he asked the waitress if she would take food stamps. She said, "I'll ask my manager." He had never even seen a food stamp. We went to a potato bar. He asked how much it cost to eat at the potato bar and when they told him, he said "What a con! I could buy a ten-pound bag of potatoes for that!" Most people thought he was serious. He had more fun doing things like that and his wife, Mom, would get so mad at him for pulling junk like that.

One night I was at the laundromat. I parked in the alley to go wash my clothes. Some guy came down the alley with a very expensive bicycle.

He said, "Give me $5."

I said, "I'll give my $5. I'll take it, but I can't get it in my trunk."

He said, "Open it," and before I could get it open, he had taken it apart and put in my trunk. I gave it to Jerry, my little brother-in-law. He marked his name on it somewhere with some marks to identify it. Well, it got stolen again and the police were not going to look for it.

So, Pop and Jerry went looking for this bicycle. They saw this kid riding it, so they stopped him and called the police over. The kid said it was his bike and the police asked Jerry if he could identify the bike. So, Jerry told the police where to look and what the letters were.

So, they took it and the police took the bike from the kid and gave it to Jerry. As comedian Red Foxx used to say, "Only in Chicago can you park and walk one block and buy your tires back."

I even had my 1964 Super Sports Chevrolet convertible stolen. I got up and got ready to go down South for a holiday weekend and walked out to where I had it parked. She was gone. I reported the car stolen. I thought I might get it back soon, but no luck. After about three weeks, a policeman informed me of where my car was. I will never forget where he said it was found. It was in Palos Heights, Illinois, west of Chicago.

I went to get it. I was really excited. I asked the guy that was working that was watching the lot. He said, "It's around back." So, I went around the building. I didn't see my car. I went back. He said, "It's out back there." So, I went back and looked really good and was devastated when I found what I realized was my car. All that was left was a body. There was no motor or tram seats or console and it was burned. I almost cried. I couldn't believe anyone could torch a car like that.

The cops came around and questioned me on my whereabouts regarding when it was taken and other questions along that line. They were asking if I was mixed up with a car theft ring. Finally, my boss told the police to leave me alone. They were coming to my workplace asking these stupid questions and wouldn't believe me when I tried to assure them I didn't know anyone involved in a car theft ring.

I knew some of the guys who were into stealing cars but I never gave any of them up. There was one time when one of the guys I know took a transmission out and had his buddy pick him and the trans up while the owner sat on the front porch. If anyone wanted or needed a battery, he would just pull up to a vehicle and take out a piece of paper and act like he was reading it while he looked the car over and then he would raise the hood and take the battery off and leave. Someone questioned him from time to time. He would say, "Joe Brown asked me to take it off and get him a new one and put it on here," while he scrutinized the paper. Then, he would exclaim, "Oh, I'm sorry I got the address wrong," or some crap. He didn't care. He had ice water in his veins.

If someone who didn't know about cars had questions about how to repair something and didn't know how or what tools and sizes they needed to take it apart and how many bolts held it on, he would be the guy to ask. Just about any car you asked him about, he could tell you all about how to take it apart. I don't know whatever happened to these guys, this guy and his sidekicks, but they knew their stuff. If you wanted a part, you would just tell one of them and within a week or so, one would call you and say, "Here's your part."

Chicago is made up of so many little neighborhoods, from slums to some of the nicest neighborhoods anywhere. One special night, I took Lynn out to dinner. I always wanted to surprise her as to where we were going. Well I took her to Jimmy Wong's, a Japanese restaurant. When we got in there they told me I had to have a tie on. Most of the time, I would have just walked out but I wanted to do something nice for my girl. You know the kind of place, it had all the little cups for sipping tea. I guess they had someone do this before so they come up with a tie. I could use it. So, I played along for Lynn's sake.

I always tried to make things special for Lynn. I guess the most lavish restaurant I ever took her to was prom night. This old country boy was for sure out of his comfort zone. We went to downtown Chicago to the Top of the Rock restaurant. We were up, I believe, 100 floors and the restaurant rotated very slowly. We could see Lake Michigan and look around and see the lights of the city. I hate to admit it, but it was beautiful. You could see the Sox baseball stadium and Comiskey Park.

It was and is located at 35th and Shields Avenue. Wrigley field, the Cubs park, was not visible because they didn't have lights until later. Lynn lived about three blocks from the ballpark. At this time, the Chicago Bears also played their games at Wrigley Field. Parking was a b**** on game days but on Sundays when the Bears played, you couldn't find a parking space. My father-in-law had a garage behind his house in the alley. He had the towing services on speed dial. If we wanted to go somewhere on game day you could bet somebody would park in front of his garage and we couldn't get out. He really loved game days.

I was living a few blocks from the ballpark myself while I was living there. My mom had sent me a shoulder to place in the oven, and I was baking it really slowly. Oh, I forgot all about it. Lynn and I went to the movies. When I got back home the oven had smoked up my apartment. The fire department was there. Well, I got booted from my apartment. The worst part was I didn't get to enjoy my shoulder. So, I moved a few blocks from Lynn's parents' house into an English basement. Lynn's little brother and I had become close. He reminded me of my own brother when he was little. We put model cars together. We even built an airplane with a gas motor. We were working on it and he finally got it built. I was helping him get it started while we were in the kitchen at the table. I got her cranked and it blew the curtains off the wall.

Jerry could put these things together in no time. Well we got her outside ready to fly and his brother-in-law, Jim, crashed it into the curb and that was all of our airplane. As he got older, we went to the movies a lot and sometimes we played pool. He was a lot younger than me but it didn't matter. We had lots of fun. When Lynn was still in high school, her school was about 10 miles from her home. I was working for a company and we had a cargo van. We delivered small parts. When I would go out and drop off some parts, I would go by Lynn's school and pick her up and drop her off at home or her sister Greta's house to babysit her nephew.

I had a great boss at my job, Artag Plastics. He never said a word to me about how long it took me to deliver the parts. I would even drive right by the office to drop Lynn off at her sister's apartment. Like I said earlier, Lynn is someone who knows what she wants and nothing can change her mind once it's made up. She wanted her mom to sign for us to get married, but that was not happening. Vacation was coming up. They were planning on going South for vacation, so I planned my vacation at the same time.

We got down to Hornbeak, Tennessee and my parents lived at or near Obion, Tennessee. We found someone to sign for us to get married. Back then, you had to have a blood test before you got married. We were busy little beavers planning how to get this done. We went one day and got the blood tests and the next day her Mom told her she couldn't go anywhere with me but finally she agreed to let her go visit my parents for the day. Well, we didn't stop until we got our blood tests and drove straight to Weakley County Courthouse. We had someone sign for us to get married. Well, we got a man who turned out to be a preacher, as well as Justice of the Peace. I thought he would never get through talking to us about the seriousness of marriage and how to be good to each other. I was a nervous wreck, but we got it over with and on the way back, we made a pact to not tell anyone we were married until school was out and she had graduated. It was going to be tough.

That night Lynn's dad had an asthma attack so they go up and left to go back to Chicago the next day. I called and asked for Lynn. They told me they had to leave for home. I was all shook up, so I cut my vacation short and went back home also. The next day her mom found out I was back in Chicago. She was mad as a hornet because I had come back home and didn't spend time with my own family.

Lynn and I just keep on dating like nothing had changed. Her parents' rules still applied and the curfew was still 11. We respected that. After we were married a long time, one night Lynn wanted to go to my apartment to clean and cook for us. Well, we cleaned the walls, mopped, etc. and cooked. We sat down to watch TV. We were both tired, so I fell asleep. I woke up and it was already after eleven o'clock.

I knew we were in trouble. We rushed out and jumped in the car. As we were pulling in front of Lynn's house, her dad was sitting on the steps. I didn't live but a block from them. If he had been able to see her on the corner, he could have seen me. I said to Lynn, "We're in trouble." We got out.

He looked at her and said, "You go upstairs," and he pointed at me, "and you go home."

I said, "Yes, sir." Boy, I wanted to tell him the truth right then. Her failure to make curfew had made her look bad, even though we were innocent. The next few days we just calmed it and by the weekend nobody said anything more about it.

Lynn's oldest brother, Bill, was back from Germany and living at home. Bill and his mom had some kind of words, so he stayed with me for a few days. I had our marriage license in my sock drawer under everything. While Bill was searching for a pair of socks one day, he found the marriage license.

I came home and I noticed he looked at me real funny. He said, "Are you and Lynn married?"

I asked him why he would ask a thing like that, so he told me he found the license. Busted! He told me, "I wouldn't want to be in your shoes when mom finds out!" Well, he was a true friend and he never told anyone.

Later on when it was close to her graduation, we agreed to ask her mom if she would sign for Lynn when school was out. We were willing to remarry if she would sign. She said, "No," so we sat on it until school was out. Lynn's high school was huge, so they gave out tickets to the graduation. Lynn only got two so her parents went and me and her little brother, Jerry, went down by Lake Michigan to the park. I was fit to be tied when they got home. I was brave.

Lynn wanted me to ask once more if her mother would sign, so I asked her and she said, "No, we're going to get her a car and she will get a job and go on to college."

I said, "That's okay, we're already married." She demanded to see the marriage license. I told her I wouldn't for fear she would tear them up. I assured her we were indeed married. So, she went to bed and told me, "If you're married, come and meet me at lunch time and we will call and if you're married, I'll bring her to you tomorrow night."

I felt sorry for Pop because Mom blamed him for everything we had done. So, the next day he called the courthouse to see if-in fact-we were married. They told him it was recorded. That night, as was promised, they brought Lynn to my house, bought our first groceries, and came over and helped Lynn put up curtains and clean house. From that day until Lynn lost her mom, she was so good to me. We had some things in common. We shared others didn't understand. She's a lot like my own dad. He didn't like some people to get close to him. One thing I know is we shared things over coffee that nobody else will ever know. I loved her like a mother and I knew she loved me. No one could have been treated any better, but as I got older I looked back and understood how she must have felt. I was older than Lynn and she was her baby girl. I'm glad she didn't, but I'm sure she should have killed me.

Chapter 7

1965, Me and The Love of My Life, Lynn

After I married Lynn, life really began for me. Everything had turned from the dark side to the brighter side. I had a good job and Lynn had also gotten a job. For the first time in my life, I felt that I could help my mom. She came to Chicago to visit. I had a sister living there so we got my mom eyeglasses and dentures. I was able to find some money to send back to her most weeks. Back in the 60's, ten bucks went a long way. Food for us was like $15 a week. Lynn was so good to me. I had someone I could depend on to be there for me and be with me. (Did I mention I love my wife?) Of course, when we told everybody we were married, we heard "Ah, I give it a year" or "It won't last long." We would show them!

The Christmas before we told the family we were married, my unknowing brothers-in-law (one was Lynn's brother, Bill, and the other was her sister's husband, Jim) took me out with them bar hopping. Sometime around 2 a.m., we went slipping into Jim and Greta's house. Bill laid on the couch and I laid down on the floor. About that time, Jim yells "They are not here. They have gone!" As a result, Greta actually left her husband and went home to her parents. Greta said to Lynn, "See how men are? I wouldn't marry him."

What she didn't know was that we were already married. It was funny in a way, I guess. They kissed and made up. She went back home and Bill got chewed out by his mom for keeping us out and upsetting her daughters.

One sister already had her son. He was just a baby. I think it was that Christmas I was talked into being Santa. If you see me now, you wouldn't believe I had to have pillows to be Santa. Several kids were there and we played baseball. Jim always had a team he coached, so there were lots of little kiddies there. I was put away in the basement while they were upstairs, and they were sending down drinks until it was time for Santa. By that time, Santa had had a few drinks and was ready for whatever.

This one little girl said, "I know you." As she was saying that I realized she knew me because I played ball with her dad. She reached up and tried to pull my beard down. It was funny trying to be Santa and not laugh. By the time it was over, my little sweet wife had to lead me home. We didn't live far, so we walked. I think I lost my pillow on the way home. I don't remember what happened to it.

After we were married for two years, we had a son of our own. Lynn told me about midnight, "I'm ready for the baby," so we took off to the hospital. It was not quite midnight so they kept waiting to check us in so we wouldn't be charged for that day. I didn't know what they were doing and didn't care about that. Lynn was hurting, so I was ready for the doctor. I didn't know I was in for the longest day of my life. I was in and out of a gown more times than you could count. Lynn would ask for me then when I got in there she would say, "I've got to pee," so out I would go again. This went on all day.

I had lunch with her doctor. He failed to tell me Lynn was having trouble with her delivery. My son, Doug, weighed 9 pounds and 2 ounces and was 21 inches long. My little wife weighed 106 pounds when she got pregnant. Unbeknownst to me, the doctor had called Lynn's mom and let her know she was in trouble but never said a word to me. Throughout my life, I think I've heard every joke about having babies ever told. One I'll never forget is the doctor comes out and asks for Mr. Jones. He asked him what he did for a living. He said, "I work for Double-Cola." The doctor said, "That's fitting. You have twins."

Later, the doctor came back in and asked for Mr. Smith and asked the same thing. He said, "I work for 3M Company." The doctor said, "Well, that's fitting, you have triplets." After a while the doctor came in and asked for Mr. Taylor and he passed out on the floor. The doctor said, "What happened to him?"

Someone said, "He works for 7-Up Bottling Company." It was funny at the time.

After waiting for what seemed an eternity, at 2:48 p.m., my son had arrived. It was right at shift change, so the nurse came by the room. She said, "You got a big boy, but don't tell the doctor. He wants to tell you himself."

I went to see him. I was so excited. His hair was black. He had his fist closed. My first thought was, he's going to be a boxer. Then, I thought he might be a football player. You know, I thought all the thoughts most dads think when they see their sons for the first time. Time flashed before me and I couldn't wait to see Lynn and then I called her mom. She had just gotten home from work and was waiting for Lynn's dad to get home so they could come to the hospital, Edgewater Hospital.

When they got there, I let her go see our big boy while I stayed with Lynn. If you become a dad and the child don't change your life, something is wrong with you. A new phase in my life was about to begin.

I used to lie in the floor with him and play with him until he could walk and by the time he walked, I had a bike and a seat on the front for him. We rode everywhere. I had to watch him because he would go to sleep on me. I would take him to visit my sister, Ludine's. She had several children and he had a time with all of them and he and his cousin, Kenny (Greta's son), grew up together. They were close when they were babies and have remained close to this day.

We didn't have to have a car seat back then so Doug always stood by me when I was driving. It took me years to not grab for him when I had to stop in a hurry. Once in Chicago I was driving and a car pulled in front of me and slammed on the brakes and I said, "You son of a b****!"

Doug mimicked me, "You son of a b****!" I had to learn that you don't do or say things around your child that you don't want him to do or say. I used to drink beer around the house. I was watching football one day and having a beer. I left it sitting there on the table. Doug came by on his tricycle and got him a drink. The next thing I knew, he was riding through the house like one of the Hell's Angels. That put a stop to the beer drinking. If you think having a child won't change you, you had better think again. I wanted so much for my mom to see our son, but it wasn't to be. She passed away before he was born. Lynn couldn't even go to my mom's funeral because she was so sick and the doctor wouldn't let her travel.

Life has funny twists and turns. All these years I lived in Chicago away from my mom and after she passed away, I lived within 10 miles of where she lived. After she passed away and I had moved home, me and Lynn would sometimes just drive over there where she lived and just sit there and watch the sun go down. There was all the peace and quiet in the world, just a stillness with a soft breeze. Sometimes that's all I needed to get a fresh perspective about things.

About the same time that my mom passed, my father-in-law's brother, James, was real sick. He lived in Michigan. Pop had gotten a call, so he and I took off up there to check on him. Nobody in the family liked his wife. She'd have you take off your shoes. Everything in her house was covered up with sheets. The way everybody talked about her, I was not very happy about going there. When we arrived, I was all ready to take my shoes off and comply with her rules while she told me, "You don't have to take your shoes off. It's okay." She liked me, I guess. Pop's brother got better so we came back to Chicago but I got a good lesson: don't judge someone based on someone else's words.

Pop's brother had three girls and one son but Pop had two girls and two sons and the two families were so different. Pop was so much fun just to be around. We were at a restaurant once and the waitress was talking with him. He decided to tease her with the "Do ya'll take food stamps" thing. She got him at his own game. She said, "No, but if you don't have money, you can wash the dishes.

"I found the money," he said. He took it good-naturedly. He was really particular about his cars. I could drive it, no problem, but I had better keep it clean. There was no smoking in his car. Once, he let a smoker ride from Chicago to Tennessee with him but he told him, If you just have to smoke, I'll stop and let you out while you smoke but you can't smoke in my car." He was a nice guy.

Once he got a car stolen and he called the police and reported it but we went out walking and found it himself and called the police and told them where it was parked.

Once we had so much snow you couldn't drive in it so he walked about five miles in a snowstorm to work. This tells you a lot about a man. When we decided to move back down South it was really hard to move away from Lynn's family. I'm sure it was especially hard on her since she had never been away from home or from her family. I just didn't really want to raise our son in the big city of Chicago. We broke the news to them. They never argued with our decision. It hurt them a lot to see us move away.

Our son was three years old. We had no idea where this journey was going to take us. We would both be starting all over with new jobs, jobs we still didn't have yet. And we were told all negative kinds of things like, "You're going to pick cotton to try and make a living." By the time we moved back down South, they had machines to pick cotton.

We bought our house in November and I moved our furniture down in December. I quit my job in Chicago and we stayed with Lynn's parents until we came down in February the following year. Buddy, one of my nephews, came to Chicago and helped me load up furniture and bring it down. This was Thanksgiving weekend. We unloaded the truck and I turned it back in to U-Haul. I spent the rest of Thanksgiving putting up curtains and setting up beds so it would look like someone was staying there.

At my previous job, lots of truck trucking companies and others were always giving me all kinds of liquor or wine, so I had two boxes of booze. While I was getting all this stuff out and packing, one of my neighbors came over to welcome me to the neighborhood and help me get things unpacked. When she saw the booze, she wanted to go get some coke and ice but I said, "No thanks."

I had to catch a Greyhound bus back to Chicago. Brownie was working for a trucking company. He had gotten me a job when I got moved back here. Well, the terminal manager got into a conflict with the owner and lost his new job. So, they hired a new terminal manager but he would not honor the commitment of the other manager, so I didn't have a job. I had a good friend working at the Goodyear tire plant and he was trying to get me on there. That's the way things were done: if you knew someone who worked at Goodyear who had a little pull, you could get a job. In this rural area, Goodyear was probably the best option. The tire company paid well and had good benefits. So, my friend was trying to get me a job. I was looking everywhere also.

I had to call my old boss to see if he would help me by giving me a layoff slip so I could at least draw unemployment. Lynn had worked for Banker's life Insurance Company as a teller at a bank. I always picked Lynn up at work on Saturday. She got off at noon so I would take my lunch break and go to pick her up at work. There was this one Saturday I went to pick her up but she didn't come out. All the people came out of the bank except Lynn. They all came out of the same door as all other doors are already locked. I waited for five to ten minutes. Nothing. So, I walked to the bank and knocked on the door. The guard walked up to the door and said, "Closed."

Where was she? Where was my wife? He said, "Everybody is gone and nobody's here." I didn't think she could have come out that door without me seeing her. I drove home and she wasn't there. I checked with her mom and she wasn't there either. So, I went back to the bank and knocked on the door. I told the guard to look to see if she was in there. He had to be persuaded, so I give him a huge cussing. He went back into the bank. In a few minutes, he came out with Lynn. She was still working away. He had to unlock the bank to let her out.

I was waiting on him for putting me through all that turmoil of worry, not knowing where my wife was. He said, "You've got to back away from the door before I can unlock it."

I had to back up to the street so I couldn't get to him before he locked the door back. Besides, he had a gun. Well back to being back at home in the South. I was steadily looking for a job. Brownie worked at that trucking company and they needed someone to type freight bills, so my brother told them his sister-in-law just moved back to Union City. Lynn got an interview with the company. Well, she got a job and I was still looking. I took my letter of recommendation to the terminal manager.

He said, "We are filled up right now," and threw the letter in the trash can. I said, "If you don't mind, I'll just get my letter back out of the trash." After a couple of weeks, one of the men working nights on the dock quit, so they called me to see if I would still work for them. I went to work one day and got a letter the next day for an interview at Goodyear. I didn't go for the interview and I can't say if I regret it or not. We never know what would be what would not be, but the trucking industry has been good to me and my family. It has had its bad times as well as great times. I think I started out at $2.75 per hour in the early 70's. I don't recall what Lynn's starting pay was. We made enough to pay for our home, food, clothes, and put our son through school. However, he started working by the time he was 16 and had his driving permit. Thank the good Lord. He was always working and has been independent since he was big enough to take care of himself.

So, I started out on the docks, loading trucks for the drivers that had routes they ran every day. When we got all the routes loaded, if there was freight left, we, as dock workers, had to deliver it after we had worked all night. I don't remember much about living back in the South for at least the first year. I worked nights and most of the next day, long hot nights and steamy hot days and since I was the low man on the totem pole, I had to work Saturdays for a half day. We had to deliver any auto parts or windshields and sometimes we had to deliver paint on Saturdays.

I worked a lot of hours. I remember going home and falling on the bed and waking up not knowing where I was. It took several minutes to figure out where I was.

The longest time I worked without going home was over 30 hours. The owner saw my time record and drove in from Memphis to talk to me. He said. "My name is WD Sartain. You need to learn how to punch in and out on your time card." He was obviously irritated.

I asked if there was something wrong. He said, "You show punching in Monday night and not punching out until Wednesday morning."

I said, "Yes, Sir, that's correct."

He asked, "You worked all this time?"

I replied, "Yes, sir, what time I wasn't stumbling around."

He said, "Why did you work this many hours?"

I told him it was because I was assigned things to do. I told him I figured they were short-handed.

He said nobody should work like that. I had to tell him what all I had done. He thanked me for doing as I was told and said, "Never work hours like that again. If you're asked, you refuse and call me. I'll take your call." We formed a good friendship that day.

Meanwhile, Lynn was working twelve hour days as well and seeing after our son. She was little, but she wasn't, and has never been, one to put off work. When her feet hit the floor our bed is made up and ready for the next assignment. Her parents taught her to make her bed and clean her room.

I read a book once written by an ex-Navy Seal and he says in the book to make up your bed every morning. He said that simple act brings success of other things in your life whether it's being a Navy SEAL or someone in the transportation business. I see the correlation with my wife. The first task of the day is to make your bed. If you make it, you've started the day doing exactly as you should. If you don't, you're starting the day by putting things off. Makes perfect sense to me.

I had two brothers and two sisters-Odie, Brownie, Ludine and Berniece-living here in the area with their families. Lynn had left all her family in Chicago. She did have some aunts and uncles and cousins in Tennessee and a great-grandmother who thought I was the only male in the family. I was assigned the bushes to trim and just about anything that came up around her house. I would take Lynn and our son Doug back to see her parents and brothers and sisters every time we had time and money. In the 70's, gas was hard to find for a while. I would take two five gallon cans and fill them up knowing how dangerous this was and if I could find gas, I had 10 gallons to get us to where we might find gas. I wouldn't do that again. God watched out for us.

During one of our trips up for Christmas or Thanksgiving on the way home it started snowing so hard and of course, Doug was standing up in the seat by me. The road was not slick so I was going pretty fast and it made the snowflakes fly much faster. Doug started crying and said, "Daddy, make it stop!" We made it home and back to work.

The hardest work on the dock with moving materials for shirts. The boxes weighed from 300 to 500 pounds with steel bands around the cartons to hold them together.

They always laid them on the floor and stacked them six to seven feet tall. They were about five feet long. If you got one of these loads on a 100-degree day with the sun shining on a metal trailer, you had yourself a job! This would also mean lots of water and salt tablets.

We had a tire company in our town. It was union, but the employees were too lazy to load tires so the trucking company loaded the tires themselves. The tire company employees had to load the tires that went on boxcars because the rail company didn't do that.

Loading tires in 100-degree weather was no fun. Some days you could fry an egg on the metal of our trailers. We had four hours to load anywhere from 800 to 1,100 tires. This would equal 25 to 30 thousand pounds on each trailer. Our drivers would load two to three loads per day. This was work in the South where there were always scorching hot summers, so for the first year or so, I worked nights loading freight.

There were some wild Southern boys working on the docks. I had been in supervision for a long time in Chicago. These boys were not supervised at night. We had a leader, but not really a supervisor. We moved all kinds of freight. One night we had a shipping container that looked just like a casket. One of the boys got up into the trailer and got into the container. The lids were never fastened down. This guy was working in the National Guard and happened to have a gas mask, which he put on. Several of the boys went into the trailer to start unloading and Larry threw open the lid and came out with a gas mask on. It scared us all to death. It was scary to me and I knew he was in there! This guy was always cutting up like a new pair of scissors.

One night he let his friend borrow his hot rod, and his friend left his convertible. His friend was an undercover cop working the college in a nearby town, so at midnight we took our lunch break and we let the top down and a bag of grass fell out, but there were no papers to roll one. The guy was nuts! He took out a brown paper bag and rolled the mother of all joints, about 8 to 10 inches long and as big as your finger. He lit this thing up and it blazed the brown paper. That was a jumbo joint and we were set the rest of the night. He didn't tell his friend about using the weed he had for sale, so when he went to sell it, he didn't have anything to sell. Was he ever pissed off!

I had a Levi Jacket I wore when I was riding my bike. I had it on one cool morning as I was delivering freight. I had a Kawasaki patch on my jacket so this older lady checked my bill and signed for the freight. As I was leaving, she said, "Thank you, Mr. Kawasaki." I almost laughed in front of her. After I got back in the truck, I had myself a good laugh.

Once, the dispatcher had me running loads of books from the printing company. The distribution center was about 70 miles one-way. I would turn about three loads per day. One day late in the afternoon, it had started snowing like crazy. It wasn't that cold, but it was sticking to the roads. In the South, God puts it down and he takes it up. I called my dispatcher and told him where I was. It was really snowing. I asked if he wanted me to make another trip. His answer was yes. Get her done, no problem. On the way back, I was going down a hill. I met a car. I saw that the driver was going all over the road, so I slowed down and just as we got ready to meet, the driver lost control and hit the front of my truck and went into a ditch. I jumped out and went to check on them.

The driver was a young lady. The door was smashed in and I couldn't get it open. Another man came up. So, he and I pulled the door open. She had some blood coming out of her hair. I tried to get her to just stay seated in her car. She looked at me. She said, "Oh Doug," as she hugged me up. "I know you. We went to school together. We dated."

I said, "No, we didn't. You got the wrong guy." We finally got her to the hospital. I checked on her until she was released from the hospital but I never heard from her anymore.

Once I was making my deliveries as I had many times before. Down the street there was a little cafe right on the corner. There was a huge storm going on. It was summertime. The rain had the limbs and leaves dropping down everywhere and my trailer got hit by a huge tree. It went down in front of my trailer and broke it. I had to lay down. Nobody was left in the cafe. They must have thought my truck had blown up. I had to sit there until the fire department came to cut the tree off my truck. They named me Treetopper for a while. In the trucking industry, we are always told all wires must be 14 feet high, so I went down this side road and the wires were too low. I took out the wires that ran into the house with my truck. I looked up. It pulled the meter and everything that was attached from the house and why this didn't start a fire, I didn't know.

Another time, I went too close to a building and knocked the wire down. It fell between my cab and landed down on my fuel tanks. I was driving a gas burner, and sparks were flying from the building. I'm thinking the wires were going to short out on my tanks. The sparks made it looked like someone set off a Roman Candle. I was ready to jump. People were yelling, "Don't get out! When you touch the ground, it will kill you!" About that time, I saw a dog run by my truck. I said to myself, "Self, it didn't kill the dog so just jump already!" I had jumped many times in my life, but never that far. I made it! The electric company turned everything off and got the wires off my truck, thank you, Lord.

There was a restaurant in a college town that had a table reserved for the truck drivers. This was one crazy group of good old Southern Boys who frequented the restaurant. We were really popular. At lunchtime, this restaurant filled up with college kids, and most of the young girls were wearing those too-short miniskirts that were in style back then.

There was a buffet, which was a college kid's idea of heaven. The kids would come and eat enough for a week and there were young ladies from all over the world in their short, short skirts. One day, the drivers were having lunch and the table next to them filled up with girls. One of the drivers knocked his coffee spoon off the table and one of the other guys picked it up and handed it to him. He said, "In the future, I'll get my own damn spoon." The next day the same guy who had picked up the other guy's spoon dropped his fork and this time the other guy caught the fork before it even hit the floor. He said, "You're just too quick. Leave my fork alone!"

Me and one of the other boys rode our bikes together. When we got off work we would ride over to the campus and watch the college kids streak. That was also a very popular thing to do back then. Once, I was dropping some friends off at the dorm. Some guy was blowing his horn and one of the windows goes up and there's a girl topless, milkshakes just a getting it. She yelled, "Wait a minute, I'm not ready." I told the guy I wouldn't put up with that. I would blow my horn again. He didn't get it so he blew his horn again and he got the same response.

One spring day, I was delivering to a motel and had to take my jacket off. I accidentally left it there. Someone from the motel called the office and reported I left my jacket at the motel. A really smart dispatcher got on the radio and announced this across the airwaves, which all my trucking buddies heard. They rode me for months. My wife worked in the office so they got a lot of mileage out of that one.

My wife also dispatched while the boss was at lunch or out making calls on the customers. My last stop was about lunch time everyday so I would call in and report that I was out at the factory. The receiving clerk was always on the dock waiting on me. We kept the radio turned up so when we were in the trailer we could hear if they were trying to reach us. The clerk who heard my wife's voice when she would call me remarked, "She sounds sexy." He had no idea she was my wife.

I said, "She is." Almost every day he would make a comment. I let it go on for weeks.

One day he said, "If you see her when you get in today, tell her I think she has the sweetest voice." I told him I would tell her that night.

He said, "Will you see her today? I said sure I will. I sleep with her every night. That's my wife." The boy's mouth gaped open. We teased him for days. The ones that knew she was my wife laughed so hard I thought they would pass out. This guy couldn't look at me for a while. I really set him up.

One of the drivers talked really funny. You would die laughing just to hear him talk. We would stop almost every morning at the bakery and have coffee and donuts. One day the owner come up from Memphis. He followed us to the bakery and wrote down what time we went in and when we come out. He met us at our trucks. One of the guys remarked under his breath that we had had it now. The owner stood there and spoke.

He asked how everyone was doing and then he asked if we knew what time we went into the bakery.

The group of us answered, "No sir."

He warned, "Well, we were in there 45 minutes. I pay you to do a day's work I expect a day's work. When you buy a dozen eggs how many do you get?"

The guy that talked so funny said, "Oh, I don't know. I don't grocery shop." I thought, This is it. We are all fired. He only gave him a long, hard look.

The man asked him if he was through with us. He added, "If you were through with us we'll see if we can get you 12 eggs." I almost fell over. I wanted him to shut up while we still had a job.

This is the clown that asked his wife what she wanted for Christmas. She said, "Oh, just get me something I can use."

He said he thought about it, couldn't come up with anything so one day he was in the grocery store and looked up to see someone delivering cases of Kotex, so he got something his wife could use. He had the nerve to ask her if she was proud of him for buying her something she could use. This man could have made a million dollars talking if he had had a good manager. Festus on Gunsmoke didn't have anything on him.

He got drunk one time in his backyard and it took him two days to figure out where he was. Once, he was crossing the railroad tracks in Greenfield, Tennessee. The tracks ran alongside the highway. While he was crossing, the light turned red so the cars in front of him stopped. It left him sitting on the tracks. The train came through, knocked the trailer off the track and hit a steel post. The funny-talking trucker got on the radio and reported that his truck had just gotten run over by the train.

The lady who was dispatching asked if any freight got damaged. He told her he wasn't sure, he was still checking himself over. He told her he was pretty sure he needed a new pair of pants though.

Several crossings didn't have warning devices back in the day. One weekend we decided to spend the night in Nashville with friends. I was tired. I got on some railroad tracks. I looked to my right and there it was, the bright light! I pushed so hard on the gas my leg cramped up God only knows how the train didn't hit us. I'm overly careful of railroad crossings now.

While I was a driver/salesman, I put weekend trips together for our customers. Once, I put a roller skating party together. We had a great time, except for the fact that someone fell and broke her wrist. There were no more skating parties. Our canoe trips were some fun times. On one of the trips we had about eight canoes with two people in each one. All day long, the canoes got tipped over, all except one. No one was turning this one over and they seemed to be having the most fun.

I started to tip them over. They yelled, "Please don't!" My question to them was why I shouldn't. Then, I saw this butter dish with a cover on it. One of them saw me eyeballing the dish and said, "Please, that's our smoke!" As I thought back, I realized maybe this was the reason these guys were so happy. I had thought it might be the beer. Nope, it was the grass. The sun was hot. The water was cold. The river was fed with springs. I threw a bucket of cold water on one of the guys. He was smoked up and it didn't bother him a bit.

Before the day was up, some of the guys, including my brother Brownie, were down to their BVDs and were diving off some of the bluffs. Brownie didn't drink much but a couple of beers had him going. We were in a van coming home. My brother didn't have a clue they had grass. Someone lit one up. He was riding up front with me and was still fuzzy from the beer. He said, "Something's on fire, pull over."

I told him it was okay and everybody was cracking up. We got back to the terminal where they had left their rides. I pulled up in front of one of the trailers and this one guy was really wasted. He looked out and saw the trailers and said, "Is it Monday already? Am I back at work?"

On one of the trips we went to Middle Tennessee fishing. We were back into the country with all gravel roads. One of our guys pulled his ski boat. While he went around a curve it slid sideways and dumped his boat. This boat was a heavy fiberglass boat. We all came behind him and it took every one of us to get it back on this trailer. Just as we did, there came the ambulance. He stopped us and asked where the wreck was. We told him we didn't know anything about a wreck. He said they got a call a boat was turned over and someone was trapped. The boat had dirt all over it but we continued to deny we knew anything about a wreck.

That night, we went out to some local bars. We went into the first one. It was pretty dark. As soon as my eyes got adjusted, I looked over in the corner where I saw that up about four feet from the floor was a big man with long hair and a beard, a rough looking dude with a shotgun laying across his knees. I was all for getting out of there, but they had a live band and the place was full of women. The guys were dancing and having a good time. I was sitting at a table with my cousin. Then there came some women over asking to sit down. They asked, "Don't you guys dance?"

We said sometimes and shrugged them off. We had a young fellow with us that had not learned the ropes. He got into it with someone outside. I got out of there. We found another joint down the road and it was packed. We were not there five minutes when some dummy came over and told me, "I'm going to cut you."

Brownie was behind him with a mug of beer. I told him, "Go on. I don't know you." He said it again. He had his hand in his pocket and said, "I'm going to cut you."

I told him, "If you take your hand out of your pocket, it better be slow because that's the last thing you're going to remember."

He stared at me and said, "Well, I'm going to cut somebody."

I told him, "It's not going to be me." He walked away. My brother has had my back more times than I can remember. I don't think we caught any fish that trip.

Later, I was going through my suitcase and couldn't find my clean underwear. I called my wife and asked her where I could find my clean underwear. She told me, "Look in the top of your Tackle Box. You didn't find them when you went fishing?" Not funny.

During one of our canoe trips, the river was up and flowing pretty fast. My wife was with me. She had ear problems, so I didn't want her to go under. We were going to hit a log in the river, so I jumped out, accidentally turning the canoe over. My wife grabbed a tree branch and held on. I went under and the current of the swift water washed me downstream. I came up and couldn't see my wife anywhere. I started to panic I went back under looking for her but seeing nothing. I got caught up against an underwater stump. It had me in its grip and I couldn't get loose.

I knew I had to free myself. I pushed so hard I tore my t-shirt. I came loose and popped up to the top and there was nobody, including my wife. I started going back up the river. Someone came down and asked what I was looking for. I told him my wife didn't come back up. I had never felt so helpless in all my life.

Someone yelled out, "There's a woman holding onto a limb floating in the water. She has a life vest on."

I remembered then, yes, she had a vest. I was so filled with joy to see that she was okay. You talk about thanking the Lord! I did over and over.

On a more enjoyable trip, I was in the water with several friends and this time the current wasn't nearly so swift. We had come down to a place along the bank where people would pull in and have cookouts and hang out, so we pulled up to the bank. We were ahead of the others.

We waited for them there and it was hot. Several people were just chilling. I'll never forget this one young lady. She was standing on the bank, just about eye level with me. All of a sudden, she started jumping up and down. Then, down came the bottom of her bikini. The bottoms were white and black and that's all I can say. During all this, my wife was in shock. Neither of us was sure what to do or say. The lady's husband showed up and she began to animatedly tell him what had happened. The story was that a bee had gotten into her bathing suit and she had shucked her bottoms off. You should have seen the look on the face of this one guy in a nearby canoe! His eyes were as big as half dollars. We laughed about this the rest of the day.

It seems no matter how much you take to eat and drink, you never have enough on the river. It's a mean river. I'm always out of one thing or another. On one windy summer day, I took my wife fishing. As we approached the watershed, I saw a young groundhog standing up and looking right into the wind. I was all the time telling my wife how I'm Indian and she can't sneak up on me.

Well, I tell her to watch me while I caught that groundhog. To my surprise, I snuck up on the groundhog. I said to myself, "Self, what do I do now?" I got the bright idea to pull my t-shirt off and grab this dude. Me and him went around and around. I yelled to my wife, "Bring me that box!" so I put him and my shirt into the box and closed it up. We lived in a subdivision, so I took him home. The neighborhood kids came over to see what I had. I turned him loose and the chase was on. The kids were after him and then he was after the kids. We almost died laughing. The groundhog was afraid of them and they were afraid of him.

On the way home from work one day we took a shortcut. My wife's parents were visiting so we were trying to get home when we drove up on a couple parked in broad daylight. The first thing my wife said was, "Look at that white butt!"

One of the guys I worked with had a heart problem. The doctor told him he could have wild meat: rabbit, deer and other wild animals. I went squirrel hunting and I killed a couple. Then, I came up on a big copperhead snake. I shot it right behind its head with a 22 rifle. I thought I'd killed it. The hunting land's owner had told me there were no copperheads on his farm, so just as my father had done years ago, I thought I would take the snake to the owner and show him. I had a Chevy Vega hatchback. There happened to be an old piece of carpet so I laid him on that. The farmer wasn't home so I carried him on over to my friend's house.

I opened the hatchback to show him the squirrels and the snake. I took my finger and ran it down the snake's back. I told him how pretty the colors were. I left my friend's house and stopped uptown to get gas. There was a man standing there. He saw the snake through the window when I got there. I told him it was a copperhead. He said, "Let me see."

I nodded. I opened the trunk. He started to reach in and the snake struck at him and almost got his hand. We had to kill it for the second time. When I was going home, I reached my turn-off and the wind caught the carpet and blew it up. For a second I thought the snake had been resurrected (again) and I almost ran my car into the ditch even though I knew I taken it out.

Chapter 8

At work, some of the guys loaded the trucks at night and another group delivered the freight during the day. The drivers came to the boss's office and decided they wanted to work nights loading the trucks and we would make the deliveries instead of them. For some reason, they didn't believe we could handle the delivery. My brother and I both worked nights. When I found out which route I had, I took the weekend and did a mock run to see where every stop would be. That Monday, I was empty by noon. We had two-way radios and when I checked in empty, the dispatcher couldn't believe it. I didn't know the other drivers before me were taking all day what had only taken me half the day. Our routes were set for unload going down the route and pick up freight coming back.

Instead of making us look bad, it backfired on the driver before me. We were driving older trucks that were kind of faded out. I had to wait until 1 p.m. to start back, so I got some wax and waxed my truck. It was red, so it really cleaned up nice. When I got it back and my boss noticed my truck, he asked, "What happened to your truck?"

I shrugged and said, "I waxed it on my lunch break." Nobody could believe I was getting my work done. There were some pets, those who received favor whether they earned it or not, working there. I went in on Monday and my pretty red truck was gone. I had been assigned a different truck. I was as mad as a hornet! I didn't say a word though. I got my wax out and cleaned that truck, too. When I was finished, I had it so slick the flies would have to wear golf shoes to light on it.

The owner of the company lived in Memphis. He had heard about how the new drivers were getting the job done and had time to wax their trucks and cut costs so he came up and rode around checking on us. He knew the other ones had been riding the clock. The terminal manager lost his job. There would be no more butt kissing and it was each to his own.

Soon after this, the owner sold out to another trucking company. We all got to keep our jobs. The new owner was just expanding his area. We were able to stay in the same terminal just as before. The new owner was looking to grow the company. We were asked to look for ways to do this. So as a driver, I started taking the shipping and receiving folks on weekend trips. I got mine paid for, so this worked out pretty good. I started taking leads from the shipping department and sending them to the sales department. Soon, we were growing our revenue.

I soon had the title of driver/salesman and my new boss was impressed with my results. It wasn't long before all drivers were called driver/salesman. I was happy doing what I was doing, but it wasn't long before my boss wanted me to be the terminal manager. He made the operation manager talk with me. I didn't really want the headache. I finally told him what it would take money-wise. He said, "We can't pay you that much. That's what I'm making after about four hours!"

The boss said to do whatever it took to make me the terminal manager. So, I moved up the ladder. Once I was terminal manager, we expanded our operation. I got out and got new operating authority so we could run into or out of Tennessee to different parts of the United States. Soon, my boss realized we could go just about wherever. So, we started a truckload division. Nobody was doing this. We began the first. Soon after, trucking companies were asking how to get into the truck load business. It just took off.

Soon, we sold the less than truck load division. This changed the whole trucking industry. Before, all freight went by class and was so rated. Glass was rated high while metal was rated at a lower cost, etc. The feds came in and deregulated all freight. Now, they rate by hundred weight. Then soon after that, we went to rate per mile. And so went trucking.

This lane was good for old Joe so he would do it for this amount. And you would have to match the rate. Someone else would do it. And on and on. My operation manager had gone on vacation and the president of the company and vice president called me into the office for a meeting and told me they had made a motion. They told me I was to become Vice President of Operations.

I said, "Wait a minute, my boss is on vacation. He should be asked about this job, not me." I wouldn't take the job until he came back and knew what was going on. They just went around him and put me in charge of operations and sales. I knew I could handle everything, except the owner because he was hard to work with. One thing he didn't know was how to treat his employees.

I finally resigned but he wouldn't have it. He wanted me to stay on as a consultant so he wouldn't lose his customers. Most of them couldn't get along with him. Sure enough, he had his secretary call me and set up a meeting. He wanted me to come back to do sales work. I would not have to answer to him. I would go through operation manager, and I finally agreed to go back.

My wife was still working there. Then, we all got together with all the sales staff, our Memphis, Nashville, and St. Louis offices along with West Tennessee. The president questioned each of us and what we had going on and the status of each account. He saved me for last, and as I went through mine, I must have had as much going on as all the others put together. After I got through, he compared my report to all the others. He said, "Here is what I need: results. Doug has more freight moving than all of you, what's the problem? He has been back for a short while, but he has things going on all around you. He has a locked-up account in your areas as well as his." You just don't do that kind of thing,

Soon, I left the company for good. The president just didn't get it. Once, after I had been gone for a while, there was some kind of meal for the employees. I went with my wife. All the drivers and office workers were happy to see me and several gathered around me talking and laughing. The owner got upset and in his little speech was telling how things were really going well and how the ones that doubted his comeback would eat crow. Shortly after this, my wife's check bounced. Again. So, she decided to call it quits after 15 years.

We both started working for another trucking company. One of the larger companies wanted me to be their general manager. I would have to be gone all the time. I didn't think this would be for me. Another trucking company wanted me for sales. During the interview, I was asked how much new business I could turn the first year. I thought about it. I thought I would give myself some room. I estimated I could generate one million in new business the first year. After about a week they called said they didn't think a million a year would be enough, so, I went to work for another company. In the first three months, I had generated $800,000 in new business. By the first full year, I had generated over three million. The company had to add new trucks and trailers to move the new freight.

The owner soon saw that he didn't want to pay the commission I was promised so I moved on. A gentleman I had hired while I was vice president over sales informed me he had gone to work for a large company. They made car seats. Meanwhile, I was in a meeting one day while I was doing sales for the last trucking company and the corporate traffic manager was in the meeting. He asked me to write up a contract as to what I would do on rates. He knew me by reputation. I told him I didn't have any trucks. He asked if I would consider buying a truck. They already had trailers. I had my own authority, but no one knew I had it. All I needed to do was to activate it with the Feds.

So, I put together a contract and in our next meeting, I was asked to get one truck for the time being. My wife and I got a truck. Our neighbor was a truck driver and had worked for me while employed by other trucking companies. As it happened, while I was getting all my plans together with my own truck, my neighbor, Jerry, walked over to my house to talk. He was going away for his annual two-week camp for the National Guard. He didn't know what I was involved in.

Out of the blue, he said, "Why don't you buy a truck? I'll drive for you for five years. I'll even sign a contract." I couldn't believe what he had just said.

I said, "I tell you what: go up to the International dealer and look at the grey tractor. If you like it, I'll buy it." I couldn't believe this was coming together for me. He came back from looking at the tractor, and said, "You're just kidding me."

I told him, "When you get back from camp, it'll be here ready for you." I kept my promise. While he was gone, I signed a contract and had the lettering and interstate numbers put on the doors. I don't think he believed me. When he came home, I had the truck sitting right in front of my house. He stopped at my house before he went home and he was like a kid in a candy store. That was our beginning.

Jerry was one of the best little drivers I've ever had and he cussed me all the time just for the fun of it. When he couldn't get me mad, he would just cuss and say, "If I can't make you mad, I'll just go home."

Once, we were in a real crowded line at a restaurant. Jerry was a short fellow and weighed about 140. I'm 6-foot and around 270. He started dancing around saying, "Come on, big boy, get you some of this!" over and over. People started to get out of line and move back out of the way. We just moved up in line. We got our food and got out of there.

Three months later, we had three more tractors and the company just kept growing. That's how Day After Day got started. I continued to work for other companies until we had maybe 12 tractors before I started working on the company every day. We saw good and bad things over the next 20 years. My wife was and is my right arm and our son was in and out of the operation. We can't say it wasn't an experience because it was. We found so much support from the people we did business with. We got our share of good advice and some not so good.

Once, Odie asked me how I managed to sleep with all those trucks out there and all the debt. I told him, "Well, I just lay down and put my head on the pillow and close my eyes."

He would ask, "Why did you build a big house with just you and Lynn?" I asked him if he would pay my taxes. He declined. That was the end of the questions.

Being in the trucking business, we had to have a lot of tires. Two of my good friends were selling tires, so they supplied us with all our tires. When you spend several thousand dollars per year on someone's product, you become important to them.

Chapter 9

One of my friends was a fellow who went pheasant hunting every fall in South Dakota. We got together with some others and planned a big hunting trip. The pheasant hunting was a new adventure for me. Everybody and his brother had CB radios back then. I think we had a three-car convoy and these guys were always pulling something on each other.

One car was out in front of us and they were telling us to come on up there, the roads were clear. One of those guys pulled over and let us pass him so he could get behind us. He then came up and started tailgating with his lights on bright. A driver got on the radio and told the guy in front of us about "this a****** with the bright lights." He said, "Slam on your brakes, that'll get them off of you!"

By this time, our driver is smoking mad. He was cursing the guy out on the radio, not knowing who was behind him. So, the guy behind us said, "Move that red truck up there if you are not going on. Just pull over and get out of my way!"

Then there was a big cuss fight going on through the CBs. Finally, when he could pass, he pulled up beside us. He was laughing so hard he could hardly drive.

We were going to stay with a family in a three-story house. It was first come, first serve. The second floor had three bedrooms and baths, with one room was reserved for a gentleman we called Papa Smurf. He had been going there for 40 years, so he had his own room.

The attic was hard to get up into. All the bunks were in one big room and we were trying to beat the others there.

We stopped for a gas break and when we came back out, the smart aleck know-it-all was behind the wheel. He offered to drive awhile, knowing we were trying to get there ahead of the others. We had been running around 70 miles per hour. We got back out on the big road. It was like we had stopped. I looked over his shoulder and this guy was driving 55.

After 10 or 20 miles, I asked him if something was wrong. He said, "I'm not getting a ticket."

I told him, "You might. I believe there's a minimum out here." This lit him up. He drove even slower. The vehicle belonged to my friend's dad. When I could, I told my friend to get this cat out or we would be the last ones there.

He said, "I'll have to use the bathroom soon as you see some place open." When we stopped, my friend ran to the bathroom like he really had to go. When the driver got out, he went inside. My friend came running back out and got behind the wheel. We were the first ones there.

We stayed in the car until the folks got up. The folks we were staying with had been farmers all their lives, growing crops and raising hogs and cattle. We took our meals with them. Their table would seat about 12 at a time. A lady and her mother would cook. They fed us breakfast and supper. We were on our own for lunch. After breakfast at nine with pancakes, eggs, bacon, sausage, gravy, biscuits, juice, milk, and coffee, you weren't hungry at noon. Anyway, I found out when the whistle blew, it was off to the races!

We walked at least 20 miles that first afternoon. We killed a lot of birds. I think we had to hide over half of them We cleaned birds for hours after supper. They were set up for it. We had a big room with concrete floors. Of course, I was the rookie so I had a job nobody else wanted.

There were some good guys and some butt holes. There were a couple of brothers from Detroit, one that was a detective and the other was not well-liked. Someone had taken his camera. He asked if we had seen his camera. Later on, he said, "Man, you guys packed a lot for one week!"

My friend asked him how he knew what we had packed. He said, "I was looking for my camera."

I told him to stay out of my room and I had better not catch him back in there. I informed him that we didn't steal. That set the stage for the rest of the week. We just didn't see eye-to-eye after that. Later on, we were sitting on a trailer drinking a Coke. I finished my can and the wind blew it off onto the road before I could pick it up.

He said, "I don't know about you, but where I live we don't litter."

I got up and started after him and my friends got ahold of me and told me to leave this jerk alone because he wasn't worth ruining our trip over. I decided he was right and we ended up having a great time.

 The farmer had a '55 International pickup truck parked in the weeds. The owner said, "That's where it quit and that's where I left it." I asked what he would take for the pick-up. He told me, "You can have it. I'll give it to you." He continued, "Do you know how many of the Tennessee boys have called dibs on it? But nobody ever comes back to get it." Well, I was no different. I didn't go back the 900 miles either.

These people were such a good family. One of our guys had a birthday while we were there and the grandchildren found out, so they had their mom and grandmother bake a special cake for him. They sang Happy Birthday to him and he was so happy. These little girls made his birthday special.

While we were out there, we went to the Missouri River. It was just a few miles from where we were staying. We stayed in Platte, South Dakota. This was amazing how years ago the river froze and pushed up waves of levees around the river. We would be just driving around on flat ground and come up on one of these levees. We saw lots of mule deer and it was exciting to see them on their pogo sticks, boing, boing and gone. With all the hunters coming into these little farm communities, it was like, "Bring your money and come on in!" To these folks, this was their cash crop during the hunting season.

The family farm where we were staying was farmed with hunters in mind. I was from the country in Tennessee, so I paid close attention through the weeds and grass, so when we were walking up to the birds, I would watch to see what showed up on the trails. Once, I was hiding out waiting and out came a big red fox! I shot him and took him to the farmer. You would have thought I handed him a handful of money. The whole family thanked me and it was the talk of the evening around the dinner table.

I found out later that that was one of the reasons they wanted us to kill the rabbits. The rabbits would bring in the foxes. Anyway, I was the hero of the hunt. The leader of the hunt brought his wonder dog. He had his dog whistle and he would blow that thing all day. One of the guys took his whistle and put it in the toilet. The next day everybody was waiting to see what happened. Sure enough, they left water in his whistle. He put the whistle in his mouth and blew it for his dog, Ranger. Water sprayed everywhere and everybody fell down laughing and the guy didn't have a clue as to why we were all laughing. At one point, he even laughed with us.

We had my friend's dad's Suburban and the last thing his dad said was, "Don't let them dogs in my seat." Well, I looked back as we got out and one of the dogs was in the front seat with his paws on the steering wheel. When you were pheasant hunting with these guys, you followed their rules: when we got to where we were going to hunt, we had to ease out, and there was no talking or making any noise. We had just taken four guys to the other end of the field to block. Now saying all that, when we had started walking, they started talking, slapping their legs, and blowing whistles. I thought the object was to chase the birds to the ones we dropped off.

One of the back doors on our ride was really hard to close. We had to push hard to get it closed so I got all ambitious and took the door apart and greased it up with WD-40 really good, so then all we had to do was lightly touch it and it closed. Every time someone got out, they slammed the door. This made our leader go nuts!

He would bellow, "I told you, don't slam the door!"

We were on our way back and it was dark. We were coming into Kansas City around midnight. We were low on gas and decided to pull off the first exit we found. The store we ended up at had bars on the windows and the clerk was in a cage with steel bars. There were people hanging out, the doors were open to the cars and people were drinking. A couple of us asked for the keys to the bathrooms but they told us something was wrong with the bathrooms. So, we got out our whistles and got on the dark end of the building and started blowing them. You've never heard anything like it! People were scurrying like a covey of birds. There were cars going everywhere and every which way. The parking lot was empty. Color Me Gone!

Then, when everybody was gone, they let us use the washroom. My two friends that were brothers called me dad. It was an acronym for our trucking company, Day After Day Service. Our customers just called it DAD'S also.

So, I'm dad with these two. At one of the stops we went into the store while someone was filling up with gas. The brothers started in, "Dad, can I have this?"

Meanwhile, the other one was, "Dad come over here! Buy this for me!" and on and on. You get the point, so I walked up to the clerk, who was working by himself, and told him, "Just watch them. Whatever they get, I'll pay for it." You should have seen the guy. He was peeking and looking at them and trying to check people out all at the same time. We drove the poor fellow nuts!

When they took their stuff up to the front to pay, he said, "Are you sure you don't have anything else?" and eyed them suspiciously."

I replied, "Yes I'm sure! What are you talking about? I don't have anything you don't see!"

The clerk had to be careful not to overdo it without proof. When it got serious, I told the clerk I was just kidding and they were just playing with me. You could see this guy let out the air he was holding in with relief.

One of the brothers looks like Jim Nabors. In fact, his nickname is Gomer. One night, we were all having supper and one of the waiters had her hands on the back of his chair. I asked her, "Do you see anything unusual?"

She said, "No."

About that time my friend let out

"Well, Gollee, I can do it! I can do it," with his best Jim Nabors impersonation.

She went into the kitchen and brought out everybody to meet Jim Nabors and the boys from Tennessee. The boys from Tennessee owned that restaurant from that moment on. When someone had a birthday, the restaurant owner would have them bring out a small cake to the table. Well, we had a birthday every night. The restaurant had license plates from all over the United States there on the walls. I had my own custom plates on the wall. We were treated like family.

Our first trip to Nebraska was during Thanksgiving. We ran into snow outside Kansas City. It snowed all night and when we arrived, all the side roads were closed down. There were huge drifts six to eight feet high. We called our farmer who had set the hunt up. He said, "I can't get out!" He lived about five miles out of town. He told me how to get to his house. We were able to get up and down the main highway, so we went looking around to see where to turn to get to his house. It just so happened a huge snow plow was going down his road, so we caught up to the plow and we were following him.

I told my friend that was driving to watch out because when the guy on the plow got too much snow in front of him, he would back up and push the snow to the side.

The cloud of snow must have been 10 feet tall and no sooner than I spoke, he started backing up. We tried to back out of his way and as we were spinning, the snowplow driver never looked back.

He was almost on top of us when we finally got traction and we barely got out of his way. Believe it or not, this happened not once, but twice. My friend is hard-headed and he didn't learn the first time. We finally got to the farmer's house. When the snow plow went by, the driver had filled his driveway with ten feet of snow. The farmer got a tractor and pushed the snow out of his drive.

I had never met the man before. He told us to get into his pickup and he would show us where to hunt. He had a cow catcher on his truck. He introduced himself as Butch and I told him my name and that I was the one who had been talking to him on the phone. I noticed he had what I thought was a handicap. I found out later it was polio from his childhood. I also found out later that, he did not consider himself as having a handicap.

As we traveled down the road where the plow had gone, there was no problem. Our guys were following us but eventually we came to a side road that wasn't plowed and the wind had swept the snow off most of the road. But as we went over a hill, we could see that the wind had left a big drift. He pulled up to it, looked it over, and he put his truck into low range and put it to the floor. We hit the snow drift and snow went 50 feet in the air. Well, we got up about halfway through the drift, so he backed up and said, "Here we go this time!" and he broke through. Meanwhile, I was hanging on and not saying anything.

We came to a plum thicket. He said, "Hunt here." Our guys were all excited, laughing while they got out of the truck and and making all kinds of noise. The pheasants started to get spooked. If one came out, I bet a hundred came out. It was 20 degrees and the wind was really blowing. It was bitterly cold. I walked about 50 yards with snow up to my butt.

It reminded me of a joke. Little Johnny was asked to make something up that rhymed, he said "Johnny went fishing. Johnny caught a bass. Johnny fell in up to his knees."

The teacher said, "That doesn't rhyme."

Little Johnny said, "It would have if the water was deep enough!"

Well, the snow was deep enough for me! I lasted for 50 yards. Everybody was telling me to come on. I told them I didn't go all the way to Nebraska to have a heart attack. The weather warmed up and the snow was melting so fast it looked like there were little rivers everywhere. It had not been cold up until the snow. We found frozen snakes. The leaves were still on the trees and the weight had broken limbs off the trees. It looked like a storm had torn the trees up.

This was a strange event on Thanksgiving Day. Nothing was open except a convenience store, where one of the guys got a breakfast pizza and in no time, he was putting brown spots all over the snow-covered land. One of our guys had never been pheasant hunting before. He came up on one under the snow and cornstalks. He said, "Hey, here's one right here!" He was pointing at it.

I said, Catch him!"

He shook his head, "No, he will bite me."

I said, "Well, kick him up!"

He did and the bird came out cackling. It was his first flush. He was normally a good shot but he was so shook up, he missed the bird three times. This was my good friend Goober. Incidentally, his brother's handle was Gomer. As the day went on, we came up on a pond with lots of ducks. Well, these country boys had to figure out a way to shoot some ducks. They snuck around the levee and crawled up on there and jumped up to shoot. Ducks fell out in the pond. Gomer asked Goober to fetch, so go fetch, he did. He went out to the pond, picked a duck up by his teeth and came out with the duck hanging out of his mouth. This was a sight to see, folks!

The farmer had a high school friend visiting from California. The man had two young boys. The younger was about eight years old and everything Gomer and Goober did, he would mimic. They taught the young boy how to put his hand under his arm and make farting sounds. His dad said, "I don't know what your mom's going to do when you get home, boys." But they didn't mind their dad very well so they probably weren't worried about what their mother might say.

One morning at breakfast, we were all around the long table. Another thing Goober and Gomer had done in their role as mentors was to get the boys drinking coffee. We were all talking and not listening to the boys. One of them said, Pass me the sugar." No one paid attention. He spoke up again, "Pass me the sugar." Again, no response. He said it a little louder the third time. He finally said, "Pass me the damn sugar!"

His Dad said, "I know you boys are in trouble with Mom!" Later, I got a report that one of the boys got into trouble at school for making fart sounds. We all hit it off and our friendships last until this day. Our wives even share the same name. We didn't find anyone out there that didn't know Butch and if we mentioned his name, we became friends right away. I love going out there pheasant hunting.

During that time of the year the Corn Huskers were playing football. Butch and I would drop off the hunters and we would ride around and listen to the game. Back then, the Huskers would run points up, forty, fifty, even sixty points. The fall weather was usually beautiful. Butch was like a long-lost brother. As I mentioned, he had polio and one arm and one leg were messed up. One fall, he got his leg caught in the corn header. The nearest Jaws of Life was miles away, so he told his farmhand to hand him his torch.

The EMT asked, "What are you doing?"

He said, "I'm going to cut my leg out of here," and he lay there and cut himself out. He lost his leg from just below his knee but it didn't change him one bit. I never offered to help him in any way. He drove a semi-tractor, combine, and farm tractors but he couldn't tell when he was getting caught up in the grass when we were hunting. We were walking through a field one day just talking and when I turned, he was gone. I looked down and saw that he had tripped. He rolled over and pushed himself up with his good arm. We never stopped talking, just like nothing had ever happened. Later, I was thinking about what just happened and I couldn't keep from laughing to myself.

One day he said he had his leg off to rest it and someone the UPS driver was outside blowing the horn on the UPS truck. He hopped over to the door. His big black dog was on the back porch. The driver said, "I have a package for you, but I'm not getting out. Will that dog bite?"

Butch said, "I believe he will. He chewed my leg off." The UPS driver threw the package out on the ground and as he pulled off, he yelled out, "This is UPS ground service!" He told us once he took and put his leg on backwards and walked in the snow and asked someone about the tracks. No one guessed what he had done. This was a guy you just had to love.

He and his friends hunted coyotes. When it snowed, they would take a flatbed pickup truck and mount dog cages along both sides with trip ropes. They usually had a light plane flying over to spot the coyotes then they would relay to the pickup where the coyotes were. They would go flying across the field with snow going everywhere. When they get close to the coyotes, they would pull the cords out and the dogs would hit the ground running, trying to get up and look for the coyotes. As soon they saw a coyote, the race was on and it was one of the funniest things you could ever see.

While on one hunt, me and Goober got the idea we would ride in the back of the pickup truck and shoot pheasant while Butch drove through milo fields. Well, the bed of his truck was slick from fuel and oil. With Butch driving, it was all I could do to hang on and it was impossible to shoot. That was just another wild idea on one of our hunts.

On another hunt, there was snow on the field and some snow drifts. Beyond this was a ridge where there was no snow Butch said, "Come on, I'll drive you guys over there. Where there's no snow, you can hunt that field. We hit the drift and got about halfway through. The pickup just sat down right there. I asked, "Butch, how are we going to get out?"

He said, "There won't be any snow here in July." Nothing seemed to bother him. He was telling us about how cold it was. He said one time he had his horses out by his house and we went out one morning and found these clear balls laying on the ground. He picked them up and took them inside while he was standing by the stove. In a few minutes, he heard pop pop pop pop. He said the frozen balls were frozen horse farts. Now that's cold!

The farmer down from Butch had International farm tractors and he also raised hogs. One Halloween pranksters caught his pigs and painted them John Deere green. He was one upset farmer. There was a place where we went to eat sometimes called Jugheads Restaurant Bar and Grill. They also played Keno, which none of us knew anything about. Some of his friends were helping us and showing us how to play. Butch always had friends wherever we went. I was playing with one of my friends with the help of one of his female friends. We played for a long time and she would get our cards to play and collect our money.

When we got ready to call it a night, we were several dollars ahead so me and my friend split the money three ways with the young lady that was helping us. She had a small son. She couldn't believe we were giving her part of the split. I remember well that she had on blue jeans. She finally took the money, folded it, and put it in her pocket. She said, "That's more money than I've had all month, and I know what I'm doing with it. This will be for my son's Christmas presents." I felt her pain. I knew where she was coming from. We bonded at that moment in time. After that every time we went out there hunting, she would come by and say hello to me and my friends.

That old saying, "You don't know me until you walk in my shoes" is so true.

We decided once to stay in a mobile home. I rented it over the phone. It was on a lake and the pictures looked good. We got out there and everyone was picking a bedroom. Brownie was on this trip, so he and I shared a room, Gomer and Goober shared one, and so on. Well, Gomer went to shower first. The water pressure was so low, the water just ran down the wall. Goober got a bucket and filled it with water, threw the water in the air, and Gomer ran under it. This is how they showered. It was a sight to see. The next morning Gomer was cooking breakfast. I had a video camera lying on the table, but no one knew it was running.

Gomer was telling us he had gone home and told his wife he had learned to moonwalk. "She said, 'You can't do that!' so I shucked my pants down and showed her!" He gave us all a repeat performance of his mooning his wife and I was about to bust a gut because I was the only one who knew it was being recorded.

On one of our trips, my son went with us. This gave Gomer and Goober somebody new to aggravate. We were going on Interstate 70 and it was cold. Goober was driving one car and my son was driving my car. Goober pulled up beside us and Gomer was mooning us. Goober let the window down quick. So, he got a cold butt for sure.

Goober and Gomer's dad was famous for his white beans. He always cooked them in a pressure cooker. One time, while he was cooking them, he told his sons to watch the beans because he had to leave for a while. Goober tried to take the lid off, but it wouldn't come off so he took a hammer and tapped it. Beans went everywhere! They cleaned up the mess and agreed not to tell their dad what had happened. One of our buddies listening to the story asked them how old they were when this happened. Gomer said, "Oh, this was last year."

On one of our hunting trips, Jerry, one of my employees, wanted to go, so I let him off to go. He was a good friend as well as an employee. He was about five feet, two inches tall and had been sitting in that truck seat for years. I was telling him we walked a lot and it wasn't easy. He told me he would walk me in the ground. When we got there, it was really cold and he was dressed for the weather. In fact, he looked like the Pillsbury Doughboy with all those clothes on and he could hardly walk. We got started. I looked around and he was stopped. I said, "Come on, keep up!"

He started cussing and said, "You're power walking!" He got mad and he was trying to keep up. He lasted about four hours. We took him back to the hotel. He had galled himself, so he laid in the bathtub for hours. His hunting was over. We did take him to play Keno. Like I said earlier, we didn't know anything about the game. Basically, you get a card with numbers and they flip the numbers around in a tumbler and draw them out. My disgraced hunter friend had his card and each time they called out a number he would cuss. When they were through, he said I can't win anything I didn't have one of the numbers!"

My friend Butch asked, "You didn't have any numbers?"

He said "No!"

Butch said, "Well, you're the winner!"

He had won $600! We were 50 feet from the number caller and this little short man took three steps and he was there! They paid him $600 and he walked around showing everybody what he won. When we got back to our rooms he woke everybody up to show them his winnings.

On this trip we had rented a small house in town. We had been messing with the shock collars. We couldn't get one to work, so I fixed it and didn't tell the others it was working. So, Gomer told Goober put it on. He said, "I'm not afraid of this collar." He put it around his neck while he was laid back in a recliner. Gomer pressed the button and Goober flipped the chair over backwards. Gomer was just as shocked as Goober. I laughed so hard I almost didn't make it.

Gomer was working for a company that had a hunting lodge in Stuttgart, Arkansas and he took me with him on a duck hunt. When we arrived, a gentleman met us at our car and introduced himself and helped us unload. He showed us to our room and took our guns and locked them up.

He stated, "We have been here almost 50 years with no accidents and we don't want to start now." This was all top of the heap. They wrote out our hunting permits and they furnished guns, shells, permits, our room and our meals, which were all with a three-time duck calling national champion.

The first night at dinner we had a fine meal of steak and for dessert, chocolate pie. I told the lady I couldn't have chocolate, so she said, "I have a buttermilk pie for tomorrow but I'll get you a piece of it."

I told her I didn't care for buttermilk, but she got it and insisted I try it. I graciously tried it and it was delicious. I told Gomer to try a bite. He really loved it and we got her recipe. This lady could cook as we found out over the next two days. The next morning, we got up and they chose to take us where we had to have waders. (Well, this fat boy almost didn't find some I could get into.) Then we took a boat back into the timber. The guide said, "We have got to put the boat here and wade the what the rest of the way."

I told Gomer, "I can't walk in mud with these heavy waders on." We stepped out of the boat and it was like I was on concrete instead of water. The water was about knee-high, no problem. We were hunting in a rice field. As we were going in, there was a noise that sounded like a helicopter taking off. Ducks covered the sky as we walked up to a fence with honeysuckle vines on it. There was a table and the guide lined us up, and put shotgun shells out for us. He sent his helper out to put out decoys. The ducks were trying to come in and light while he was out there. Meanwhile, our guide gave out instructions about when to shoot and reload. He called all the shots.

I believe shooting time was 7 a.m. There were eight of us, so we could carefully kill four a piece. As we were shooting, the guide's helper placed the ducks behind each of us. By 7:23, we had our limit for the day. We went back to the lodge for a huge breakfast. We had the rest of the day to ourselves, so we rode around checking out the ducks and geese.

Stuttgart, Arkansas is the rice capital of the world. We came up on a field of snow geese, thousands of them. While we were parked watching them feed, we saw two guys get out of a pickup truck. There was a deep ditch between the road and the geese. The geese were feeding toward the road. These guys came up the ditch and crawled to the top of the bank and just laid down. When the geese cut right up to the ditch, these guys jumped up and when they did, the geese started getting up. By the time the geese were eye level, they started shooting. I had never seen anything like this in my life. Geese were falling all over the place.

They went and got their pickup and went out picking them up. We drove down to where they were, so they had to run down the ones that weren't dead. When they got all of them picked up, the truck bed was full. I don't know how they knocked down that many with ten shots. However, I jump shot some ducks once and I picked up one that couldn't fly. When I dressed it, there was no shot. He had broken his wings getting up. By the way, there was no limit on snow geese.

The next day we went back to the same place we were the day before and it was the same routine. We all shot and reloaded and maybe 30 seconds after we reloaded, one of the guys pumped his gun. The guide said, "Step back. Is there a problem with your gun?"

 He told him no.

"You reload when everyone else does," the guide informed him. The second day it took longer to get our limit, every bit of seven more minutes. By 7:30 we were on our way out for another fantastic breakfast. I saw how celebrities live. This was the safe hunt of a lifetime. I thank my friend Gomer for taking me and making more memories.

Probably one of the most memorable hunting trips we ever went on was to Ranger, Texas to go quail hunting.

Again, Gomer put the trip together so Gomer asked one of our friends, J.A., to go with us. We got to some small town outside of Ranger, Texas where we were supposed to get a key to the gate. We followed this gentleman to the ranch. He got out to open the gate. I noticed him strapping on a gun. The gate was locked with ten locks. Every other link on the chain was held by a lock.

There was a long driveway up to the house where we were to stay. When we got up to the house a stack of plywood was on the front porch. One of the pieces had blown out into the yard. Our guide went over with a stick and he flipped the plywood over. Then, he picked it up and put it on the porch. We went inside and he used his stick to flip over the throw rugs. He lifted up the bedspreads and looked under the beds and beat on the pillows. I said, "You looking for something?"

He said, "Rattlesnakes."

I told my buddies, "I'm going to get a room uptown." We all agreed, but before he left us he told us not to get on our four-wheeler without checking them because the snakes would crawl up inside where the engine was warm. Okay, no problem. He also told us if it didn't stick sting or bite, it was a rock. I had heard that somewhere before.

The next morning, we were at McDonald's having breakfast. As I sipped my orange juice, I noticed it ran out the corner of my mouth. I wasn't in any pain so I just ignored it. As we got out to the ranch, we got our dogs out and I put my whistle in my mouth. My dog was running around, happy to be out, so I blew my whistle and it fell out of my mouth. I didn't know what was going on. I rode down to Gomer.

He looked at me and asked if I was okay. I told him, "Yeah." He called our friend over.

He came up, took a look at me and said, "We have to go. You have had a stroke." I told them, "No, I feel fine. Let's hunt."

I now know they couldn't enjoy the hunt. We couldn't find any birds. The guide had told us there were some guys cutting mesquite and if they came running, it would mean they had run up on a big rattlesnake. We never saw a snake and saw very few birds, so we cut the trip short and headed home. By then, my speech was slurred and my eye would not close. I couldn't wink at the waitress when we stopped on the way home in Hope, Arkansas to spend the night.

I couldn't lay down because the pressure hurt so bad. They were calling me and asking if I was okay. Finally, I took the phone to bed with me and took all pillows and tried to sleep sitting up. I had both of the guys upset with me because I wouldn't go to the hospital. As we got into Memphis, Gomer made me call the hospital and tell them I was on my way and would be there within two hours.

I had taken the toe of my shoe and dug up a small cactus before we left from out there. I had thrown it on our trailer. I don't know how it stayed on, but it did. Our dog boxes and four wheelers were all on the trailer. As soon as we pulled into my yard, they unhooked my trailer and said, "Go now!"

Well by then I was a little worried myself. The doctor and nurses were waiting on me to take me right back to run tests. The doctor on call was from another state. He took me in a room and said, "I've got good news and bad news.

You didn't have a stroke all right, but the bad news is you got Bell's Palsy and there's no cure."

I told him, "No, my grandmother had palsy and she shook."

He said, "No, this is not the same." Anyway, I hope nobody ever gets Bell's palsy. It's very painful and nothing seems to help. My sister-in-law is a nurse. She told me to take my fingers and massage my face, so I did but one day I told my wife to get me some Vicks salve. She did and I covered my eyes really good and massaged the mix into my face and neck. I did this for three days and after that, I could wink with my eye and my face went back like it was. I know I had people laugh at me but it worked on me.

On a side note: the cactus is still going. This year, it bloomed with beautiful yellow blossoms.

I don't believe this has been done before but one year, on the opening day of deer season, me and Hubert went to another area to hunt. Hubert and I had built a deer stand on a farm where we were allowed to hunt. So, he hunted the stand and he killed a buck. Then, I came along as he was taking the deer out. He told me to go and get into the stand because the deer were really moving. I went and got into the stand and along came a buck. I shot him. I was dragging him out when Brownie pulled up and I told him the story of how Hubert had killed a buck and I had also. I told him where the stand was and he went and got into the same stand. Within a couple of hours, along he came, dragging out a buck. Three brothers on the same day in the same tree stand, each one killing a buck. It has to be a record of some kind.

Once, we were out in Nebraska pheasant hunting. On this trip, we had some dogs that would not obey so we had shock collars on them. One of the dog owners was trying to get his dog to come hunt for him. He shocked his dog. It ran over by my friend Jay and got up against his leg. Jay was hollering, "Get the dog off me! Turn it off! Turn it off! Turn the damn thing off!" The guy that was doing the shocking couldn't see Jay. Then the dog started coming to us and we ran all over the field. All the dog knew was that he was hurting and he was looking for help.

That year the weather was hot. We hunted in t-shirts that were soaked in sweat. After walking through the hot milo fields, Goober looked over and said, "I think my water just broke." My two friends are going to have fun wherever they are. We went to the grocery store to get our food and Goober climbed into my shopping cart and begged me, "Dad, get me this," or "Give me that." They had a phone on a post in the middle of the store. Gomer said, "Dad, phone for you." He was holding it out for me.

I took it and said, "Hello? Sure, I can do that. When do you want me to handle this job for you?"

Meanwhile, Goober is still asking, "Dad when are we going home? I'm hungry." There was this lady watching all of this. She came over to us and asked where we were from. We proudly answered her that we were from Tennessee.

She stated, "You need to go back to them hills. You don't belong out in the public!" We laughed at her but she was dead serious.

One of the clerks got a camera out of the stock and put film in it and started taking pictures. She said, "My boss will never believe this!" When we were finished, we went outside and there was one of those pony machines you put a quarter in and ride on. Goober put a quarter in, turns his hat around backward and climbed on the pony. The clerk came outside and snapped a picture. After we were gone, we later found out that the picture somehow ended up in the newspaper, along with whatever the clerk had told them.

The weather was crazy hot and on the way home, we ran into storms. Gomer pushed the gas to the limit. We learned that when his dad's car is on empty, it's empty. We ran out during a storm about a mile from the exit where we could get gas. Well, they had me go for gas. I don't like lightning. I walked up there to get a five-gallon gas can filled up. I looked up and Gomer had found someone to pull him up to the pump. Man, I was P.O.'d!

"Yes," I said, "here is your gas. You pour it in!" The most cherished hunting trip I ever had was when my son and older brother went with me to Nebraska. My son has never been a hunter, but he was with us. I got to witness his shooting pheasants. He, like me, loves dogs. He worked with my dog.

We deer hunted a few times but he just couldn't see himself killing the animals. Once, we went rabbit hunting. I saw one sitting in a patch of grass. I told my son to just shoot the nose so he didn't spoil the meat. I walked on and he didn't shoot so I told him, "Shoot that rabbit!" He told me it had gotten up and ran away. I walked back and there it sat. I said "Shoot it!" Boom. There was nothing but a ball of fur left.

On one of our special hunts, a youth could kill a doe. He let me know he wasn't shooting a baby deer. I told him that was okay. I said, "They will come right through here, so watch." Sure enough, along came several deer with one being a very small deer. We would be shooting downhill, so when he lined up with a big doe, he shot the big deer. It ran and the little one fell right there.

He said, "See what you made me do!"

I said, "There is no way you shot that deer. He went tracking the one he shot. I was inspecting the little one. I looked on one side and there was not a mark on it. I took it by the ear and turned it over, no mark. I did this for twice. Three times. No mark. I turned the ear loose and I had blood on my hand. My son had shot through the big doe and had hit this deer in the ear. About that time he yelled, "Here she is!"

On these special hunts you had to harvest the ovaries and turn them in when you checked in your deer. He only had one permit, so we had to leave the little one. While I was collecting the samples, he said "She better not have babies in her."

I told him she didn't. He was very troubled by what had happened and I didn't want to make it worse. She was with twins. If he reads my book, he will know he killed four with one shot. He never went deer hunting again.

As far back as I can remember, me and my brothers always hunted on Thanksgiving morning. We hunted rabbits for many years, then deer were brought into this area. From then on, we hunted deer on Thanksgiving Day. As I lost my brothers one by one, it was down to just me and Hubert. We kept going until I lost him a couple of years ago.

Never in my life has there been such a loss I felt as completely as when all my brothers were gone and I hunted all alone. It will never be the same for me. I find my interest in hunting is not the same. I still love the outdoors and all God's creations. The void of my brothers and not being able to share my stories with them has made me realize that life is just a vapor. So many times, I find myself wanting to tell them about my hunts and the deer I have seen or shot. When I lost my brothers, I lost my zeal for hunting. And losing my last brother was the hardest. Friends never fill the void of your family. Love them while you can and hang on to those memories.

Gomer and Goober fetching ducks.

Goober, one of my best friends.

My son, Douglas, looking like he's posing for Field and Stream.

Like father, like son. Our first pheasant hunt together in 1995. Superior, Nebraska

Chapter 10

My son was always very obedient. We thank God we never had problems with him being into drugs or alcohol. He was and is very independent and dependable. I am so proud of the relationship he has with his mother. I have never heard him even say anything short to her. One Saturday I was cleaning the car. I was washing it and saw the battery cable had some corrosion on it, so I took it off and cleaned it and placed it back on, but didn't tighten it up. My wife came out and took the car grocery shopping. Our son was playing with my neighbor's kids. My wife called and said the car wouldn't start and I knew right then what I had forgotten to do. I told her I would be right there.

I called my son and told him to come on so we could go start his mom's car. As I was putting him on the back of my motorcycle, my Dad pulled up. He asked where I was going and he told me to leave his grandson there with him while I went to start Lynn's car.

I asked my son if he wanted to stay with his granddad and he said yes. I was almost to where my wife was when I came to a red light, where a car turned in front of me. I went up in the air and came down off the guy's trunk. My bike was totaled. I lost a tooth, busted my watch, ripped my Levi's all the way down one leg, and messed up my knee for life. All I know was God sent my dad to my house. If not for him, my son would have been killed if he had been on the bike with me. I didn't know what God was telling me then.

When our son was three, he was playing at our friend's house with their children and he ran into the bathroom and tried to stop on a rug. It slipped out from underneath him. He hit his head above his eye so hard on the toilet bowl, it busted the skin. He came out saying, "I need a Band-Aid." Blood was everywhere. Our friend grabbed him since she saw him first. Out the door to the hospital we went. He had to get sewn up and they put a cover over his face. He could not stand for it to cover his mouth and nose. He took that after me. He wanted it moved. They had him strapped down and that was bad enough, but then to cover his mouth was too much. I took and moved it so he would calm down. Sure enough, he started to settle down. The doctor put it back and he started crying again, so I moved it.

The doctor was sewing him up and he put it back over his mouth and Doug started screaming, "Take it off! Take it off!" I moved it again and looks the doctor in the eye and I said, "Don't put it back." He didn't and our son had a black eye for months. I was worried for a long time his eye didn't look right.

One of my son's best friends is the daughter of the lady that carried him in her arms to the hospital that night. He was so bloody but she would not give him to his mother.

My wife is one strong person. A day or two before I was to go to Nebraska hunting, I discovered a small lump in one of Lynn's breasts. I brought it to her attention and she promised to get it checked out. After I returned, she got an appointment and we went to the hospital for them to check it out. I thought it was a benign cyst. I waited for Lynn and watched TV in the waiting room. Lynn's doctor was a woman. She came in and asked me to go into a small room.

She said, "It's cancer." Just like that. I will never forget that feeling. I felt like I had been kicked in the gut by a horse. Every hair on my body was dripping with sweat. I couldn't absorb what she was saying. It felt like an eternity until she said, "If it has to be cancer, this is the "good" kind." I didn't know what she meant. All I heard was "cancer." She also told me she took it out and it seemed like she had gotten all of it.

We went back to her office on Monday and as she checked Lynn, she kept saying, "It seems like I got it all, but you might want another opinion." I had already checked on a doctor in Nashville at Vanderbilt. I was checking him out. He was a surgeon for breast cancer. I went as far as to ask his nurse who she would see if she needed a doctor for breast cancer. She didn't hesitate one second before telling me. As it turned out, we used this doctor.

In my life, I had faced hunger, humiliation and pain. I had lost my mother, my dad and a brother, but this was an awakening. It can't be explained what happens to you when someone has told you the love of your life has cancer. Lynn made the choice to have surgery, so we stayed in Nashville until the doctor could see her that next week. After that, we came home with the tubes and all. I knew her body was weak but she was so strong and brave. During one of the trips back to Nashville–I think it was to get the tubes out–we went to Opryland to see the Christmas lights and shows. She was always upbeat and I always tried to hide my emotions.

She put her faith in our Lord Jesus Christ and never wavered once. For several years, the Lord had tried to get my attention, but I just let it go by. This time my heart got ripped open. I accepted my Lord and Savior and have been so blessed to have done so. That was a new beginning for me and I wouldn't take anything for that. I praise him every day for my life.

After Lynn got the tubes out and we were home, she started treatments. They made her so sick. She would ask for something to eat. I would fix it and take it to her and she would tell me to take it away because it was making her sick. This went on as long as she was taking chemo. I got up and got ready for work one morning and as I turned around to tell her if she needed anything to just call, she was dressed and ready to go. I asked what she was doing.

She stated matter-of-factly, "I'm going to work"

"Oh no, you're not!" I argued. She was determined and I finally relented.

I said, "Okay, let's go." We got a mile or so from home before she told me to pull over. She got sick and I brought her back home. Up until that point, I had only seen her cry since being diagnosed with cancer just one time for about two minutes. She had said, "I'm so young," and hadn't cried again until this day.

She said, "I want to go to work." She cried more because she couldn't go to work than any other time. She might be a small woman but she has more grit than most men. We went through every treatment together and I never missed a doctor visit. We had our own little thing. As soon as she walked out of the doctor's exam room, she would give me a thumb's up. I know we were blessed with travel safety and care.

She was soon back at work and has never slowed down. It's been over twenty years. She has worked in the

American Cancer Society for years. Then, we had some helpful-minded ladies that looked and saw a great need for our cancer patients here in our county. Bless these fine women. Lynn has been on board with them since day one. This year marks twenty years. I think if they passed out awards for selflessness and determination, she is my winner. Look in the dictionary for determination and you will find a picture of Lynn.

Not only does she work doing all she can for others, she also has helped our trucking company grow and prosper. I could not have made it without her. She is my rock. We have also had some great employees over the years that became like family. I want to try to name everyone, but I might forget someone. I will say the when the first employee we ever had passed away, one of our drivers drove his truck in front of the funeral procession. He used to say, "When I die, just roll me into a ditch. Nobody would come to my funeral." Well, we had a line of trucks and cars four miles long.

I thought back to what he had said and I laughed and told him, "Look, little buddy, they are stopping traffic for you." We all miss him very much. I often tell drivers what a performer he was. When drivers were late for their appointment his saying was "Keep the left door closed and you won't be late," or he might use his special phrase, "I could have backed up all the way and not have been late."

I had one driver that was slowly losing his eyesight and the day came when his doctor told him he couldn't drive over the road anymore. He came into my office with tears in his eyes. I asked what was wrong and what happened. He said, "I have to give my notice. I can't drive anymore." That's more than just an employee. That's dedication and we had many over the years, good folks like him, who helped us be successful. We had a fleet of 40 power units and 118 van trailers and 3 Hotshot trucks.

In our support for the American Cancer Society, we sponsored golf tournaments and I got started playing golf. I would try and pick really good players because they had to carry me. I had played about nine times when I went to an auction and bought some Woods at the sale. On one particular day, one of the guys I was playing with happened to be Gomer and he didn't mind helping me. They told me to lead off. I think it was a par three, 143 yards. I took out my driver and Gomer asked, "Have you got a 3 wood?" I told him I did. He told me to use it. I teed up and took a swing. It hit right in front of the green and rolled up a hole in one.

The green was set up so that if you went off the back it was straight down. I said it went in, but no, it didn't. It went off the back. All three of my teammates were good golfers, but not a one landed on the green. I couldn't wait to get down there! Gomer was driving our cart. I saw where the ball had rolled in the dew straight into the hole. I wouldn't go on the green until one of the guys came over. When they did, everyone was yelling. The other team behind us told us to shut up. We won our flight and every year after that we won. Once we won and got to go to the Legends in Nashville. Now, that's a golf course, but we didn't win up there.

Even though there are long hours and grief and considering you can never go home and leave it because it's with you all the time, trucking has been good to us. We have had drivers hit deer and once someone even hit a black bear in Wisconsin. You are always on alert in trucking. You only get out of it what you put into it, but that's with whatever you do. You must give 100%. As my friend would say, "I'm going to have fun, even in church."

Chapter 11

This was me around the age of 35.

On one of our hunts to Nebraska, my friend Butch asked if I wanted to ride uptown and I said, "Sure." When we got up to the main street, there was a company there that engraved rocks. Around that area there were huge rocks with addresses and names of the businesses all around. Butch slowed down and the sample rocks were lined up for a couple of blocks. We were going really slow and he was telling me to look at this one or that one. All of a sudden, I saw a rock form close to the outline of Tennessee with Day After Day Service with a truck in the background.

I said, "Hey, stop! Someone has stolen my company name!" He laughed and said, "I ordered that for you. I just gave him a picture of a truck and your name. I didn't tell him you were from Tennessee. He just chose that rock." I couldn't believe my eyes! We had only known each other for a short time, but that's the type of friendship we had developed. He is a very special friend.

My friends Gomer and Goober invited me to Kentucky on a waterfowl hunt. Goober and I went together. The spot where we were hunting was flooded by man with a levee. Goober had a three-wheeler so we both got on it and headed out to the pit. It was dark, but we had a beautiful, almost-full moon. As we started up the levee, the three-wheeler reared up. I was on the bottom and Goober was on top of me. He was smashing me. As we laid there not able to get up, we looked like turtles on their backs. He was laughing as we were both trying to get up. I looked up and it seemed that even then moon seemed to be laughing at us.

We made it to the pit and got it all set up. Then, a mallard Drake came up by himself. They called him as he was circling. They said, "We're going to let you kill him." Well I was on the spot I couldn't miss. As he got close enough, they said, "Get him!" I pulled on him. Bang. He folded like a dish rag.

Then they announced that duck season was closed. They informed me we were there for geese only. They told me I had better get out and hide that duck, so one of them jumped out, got the duck and hid it under a goose decoy (shell). Well, about that time a three-wheeler was approaching from across the field.

One of our guys was looking through field glasses and said, "It's the man. Make sure you have your license and plugs in your guns and make sure your shells are all steel shot, no lead.

They got all shook up. The guy showed up and started looking through our decoys. He didn't have a game warden's uniform on, but I figured he was undercover. The next thing I knew, he walked over to the goose shell. He stood there looking at it and then flipped it over, revealing my duck. By then, I had figured it out. One of them had made him wise for him to know what happened. I was the joke of the day.

One of our best hunters and a good friend could call and shoot and kill high flying ducks better than anyone I have ever seen. We always cooked and ate good in the duck blind. And this friend could go to sleep faster than anyone I have ever seen. He could be snoring and his brother would be calling ducks and when they got ready to shoot, he would get up, shoot and kill ducks and sit back down and start snoring again, all within a minute. It was unbelievable how he knew where the ducks were in the first place.

I asked him how he knew when to shoot and where the ducks were. He said he could tell by the way his brother was calling.

Where they hunted was state-controlled. You had your spot but if you weren't there in your blind by shooting time, someone else could hunt your blind. Once when he was young, he and his dad had started out and the boat quit on them. By the time it was up and running, some men had gotten in their blind. His dad told the men it was his blind and he would put his boat over in the grass and for them to pick him up. One of the men told him no and that they were going to hunt this blind today. He asked how many were in the blind. They told him it didn't make any difference because they were hunting it and he needed to leave.

Well he had hunted the lake all his life and been through all kinds of deals. So, he asked one last time. The answer came back the same: they told him they were hunting there today and he was not hunting there today. Our friend's father said to him, "Put your gun on this blind. If anyone points a gun over the top, shoot him. He reached over in the boat, got his can of gas and started splashing it onto the blind. He said, "If we can't hunt, you can't either." As he reached for some matches in his hunting bag, they were begging him not to light it. They said, "We're leaving right now."

Anyone who's a lake duck hunter will understand. There have been more lightning strikes that have burned blinds than I care to talk about. Some even got blown up. There is a lot of time, money, and hard work that goes into a good duck blind. So, you see why a hunter feels as if it belongs to him. Reelfoot Lake is a hunting and fishing paradise. It can be very dangerous with the stump infested water. Some well-known sportsmen have drowned at Reelfoot Lake.

Gomer, Goober and some other friends had a duck hunt planned one Saturday. They were to go on out and take our supplies and take other hunters out to the blind. I was to pick up our friend, the local veterinarian. I got up and ready. It was foggy but I made it to pick up our friend. When we arrived at the lake, it was so foggy we couldn't see. Meanwhile, Gomer and Goober had left the blind, heading to pick us up.

After a few minutes, they stopped the motor to listen and one of them called out, "Can anyone hear me?" Goober's brother-in-law, Harold, informed them they were still at the blind, so they pointed the boat in the right direction and started out again. We were waiting on the shore for them. They came within 100 yards of the shore. We could hear them talking and going right up the shoreline. This went on for several minutes until they stopped and turned the motor off. They could hear us so they came toward the sound. Finally, we made it to the blind. See, they had markers going out to the blind. We could hear ducks flying but couldn't see them and they couldn't see us. Finally, as the fog lifted a little, we killed several ducks. By the time we saw them they saw us, it was too late.

The only time weather worse than the fog was the time we had to break ice to get to the blind. By the time we got there, I was a wreck from that sound. I will never be a part of that again! Gomer said, "Any more ice and I'll be home watching TV." You betcha.

On one of our vacations Goober and his wife went with us. We had a blast. I think we went into or through nine different states. Mount Rushmore was the highlight of our trip. We did a drive-through zoo. As we entered, I had my window down. All of a sudden, an ostrich had his head inside the car, right in my face. My first thought was to let the window up but then I told myself that if I did that, he would beat my car up with his feet. These birds are huge! We were slowly moving along and he was walking with us. Finally, he took his head out of the window and I put it up and kept it up for the rest of that adventure.

We went over to Deadwood, South Dakota. This was a small town where Wild Bill Hickok was shot. The streets were lined with shops and bars. Our wives were shopping and me and Goober were checking out the bar when we came upon some guys and gals dressed like the folks in the 1800's. The men had long white, or in this case, dirty coats. One of the biggest men I ever saw walked into the middle of the street with a bullwhip and popped it. It sounded just like a shotgun. Their hair was long and dirty-looking. I don't think any of them owned a comb.

We must have been staring. One of them said, "What are you looking at?" One of the women reached over to one of the guys and put her hand in his hair and said, "Here, you want some lice?" She made a motion to throw them on Goober, so we went outside where this big man was with his whip. When our wives returned, we asked him nice to pop his whip so they could hear it. He said, "Grab that rail and I'll pop your ass." I believe these were the dirtiest and most hateful people I have ever encountered. I guess they were trying to live up to Deadwood's reputation.

Goober told me. "Let me get on your shoulders and give me that 2x4. I'll smack him!" I told Goober that the man wouldn't even feel it. In this case, we got the heck out of Deadwood. We got down to Del Rio Texas and crossed the border into Mexico. You talk about border towns! This was new for me. Kids were trying to sell gum, running around just in panties. This was heartbreaking. As we walked down the street with our wives, some pimp was trying to sell his sister upstairs for fun. He kept telling us to come on. I had to tell him to leave us alone.

As we were leaving Del Rio heading to Dallas, Goober was driving. As we came up on this car, he pulled over to the right side. Goober said, "This guy is drunk." So, he backed off him so he pulled back out in his lane and we caught up to him again. He pulled over again. He had been driving okay, so we passed him. We come upon another car and it was the same thing. We passed him. We came up on another pickup and again, the same thing: they pulled over, we passed and they came back out in their lane.

Goober liked this: no more blinking lights to get someone to pull over. We done this until we got close to Dallas. That was the end to folks pulling over. Instead, they would try run us over.

During one hunting trip, Goober was driving through Kansas City while drinking coffee, eating a donut, and talking on a CB. We didn't have a cell phone back then. Gomer asked Goober, "You got your hands full. Who's driving?" I told him not to ask. I told him to just close his eyes and we would be in Nebraska before he knew it. We had been out there in ice, snow, and everything in between. This year was hot and as dry as snuff. The dogs couldn't smell. We hunted in t-shirts.

I loved the people out West where we hunted. It was like walking back in time 50 years. We had people drinking coffee with us and asking what we were doing out there. We would tell them we were hunting and they would say, "I got a section five miles north and you can walk my farm." These were great people. We stopped at a little store with one fuel pump. A lady had pulled on one side and we pulled on the other side. We waited for her to fuel up. She told us to go ahead but we insisted and helped her fuel up. She asked what we were doing out there. My friend told her we were turkey hunting. She said, "We have a farm and we have turkey. Follow me and I'll show you where you can hunt." We arrived and she took us out to their shop and introduced us to her husband and son.

She told him we were going hunting. The husband said, "Okay. Just go down this little road to the farm." So nice.

We went to another farm to ask about hunting. They were having lunch. Some of the guys with us were young. As we entered the house, I took my cap off while I was talking with them. When we left, one of the young guys asked why I took my hat off. I told him, "You respect these people and their home." Needless to say, they told me go ahead and hunt but not to shoot any hen pheasants.

 I told them we didn't do that and that we hunted legally. It was like this when I was a kid, people trusted you. In these small towns it doesn't hurt when you got a local man that has lived here all his life and well liked. My friend Butch knows everybody for miles and we never met anyone who didn't know and like him. There was a hardware store where we get our license each year. One year we were late getting out there and as we went in to get our license, they started laughing and saying they didn't think we were going to make it. One of them said, "So happy to see you." These folks truly are American.

Some of my fondest memories are taking young sportsmen on juvenile deer hunts. The son of a dear friend wanted to hunt with me and another good friend who had some young hunters himself, so we agreed to take the boys hunting in the a.m. I took one of the youth and we got our deer. It was his first kill and it was so exciting for him. He talked to one of the other young hunters who didn't get one during his morning hunt. In fact, he had had an accident while hunting with a single shot shotgun. He had been trying to aim and laid his face over the hammer. As he pulled the trigger, the hammer cut his cheek so he had to get some stitches.   —

After coming back, I told him I would take him that afternoon if he would lie down and rest for a while. After his nap, I took him and had him work with me and my gun because it was an automatic. After I felt comfortable with him, we talked and he told me everybody had told him he couldn't kill one his first time hunting.

I tried to encourage him. I don't know why I told him this, but I was trying to get him hyped up, so I said, "We will get you a deer this afternoon. I'm a professional deer hunter." So, we got out in our tree stand. I stood up and let him sit on my feet. It wasn't a good set up at all. There was a mound of dirt in front of us. Soon after we got there, I heard a deer coming, so I got the boy's attention and pointed out where the deer was coming from. There it was. He shot and it down it went.

I reached down and took possession of the gun. He jumped out of the tree onto the dirt mound. Jumping up and down, he said, "I got that SOB! I got that SOB!"

I said, "Boy, what did you say?"

He started mumbling and we loaded up our kill and headed to the country store where we all stopped in for gas, sandwiches, and cold drinks. There were fifty guys there. My hunter was really happy he got one. One of the men asked if he got him a deer.

He answered, "Yes, Sir. I was hunting with Doug. He's a professional deer hunter." I thought I was going to pass out. These guys laughed at me for days. You know how friends are, they would ask my advice on this and that. The moral of the story is watch what you tell young people. It will be repeated for sure. It's exciting to see these young hunters experience the anticipation and the sheer happiness at just seeing a deer walk out. Heck, it still gets my blood pumping when they appear out of nowhere.

I really enjoyed all the hunting I got to do with my brothers and friends. I guess down South life is just much simpler. It doesn't take as much to entertain us. All the gravel roads we rode watching for wildlife with a box of cookies and a coke in the seat between us. Oh, and all the stories. Sometimes they would take us back to our childhood. Sometimes we would revisit our dreams. And sometimes we could talk for hours with "Do you remember when ____?" Priceless.

My oldest brother, Odie, could play music sing and write songs. I still have some tapes he made for me. I had the privilege of working several years with my older brother, Brownie, next to me we were very competitive, all four of us brothers, but as they say down South: when it came to the nut cutting, you kick one of us and you just woke up the rest of the pack. So many times, my brothers were there for me. I only hope I was there for them. I have lost all three now. That just leaves me and my sisters. For so many reasons, I'm proud of my family. Just knowing what we've come through is a miracle in itself. As I look back, which I try not to do because of where I come from, everything I've been through has made me a better person for it. I'm just a simple person with common sense in a world where common sense is uncommon.

Well, I told you I would talk some more about getting married in the courthouse and not giving my wife a proper wedding. We both were foolish at the time. I guess it didn't matter then. And I told you we were told many times it wouldn't work. Well, last year marked 50 years of marriage. As our anniversary approached, I started talking about renewing our wedding vows. Lynn didn't say much as we were getting closer to the big day. I asked her if she was going to do it or not. We had to plan. Some of the ladies at church told me they would do anything I wanted them to do. Knowing they were eager to help and talking about it got me a little excited about the whole thing.

I told Lynn these ladies had everything started. One was in charge of the planning, one would do the cake (and oh, so good was the cake). I came home after talking to the our church friends and told Lynn she better start calling her family so they would have time to plan. All of a sudden, she got excited and got going! The next thing I knew, she had bought her wedding dress. I told her we didn't get it right the first time, so we would do it right this time.

I called my dearest friend, Brother James, and asked if he would perform the ceremony and he said yes. Before I was through asking, he had said yes. He and his family have been great mentors. So, we had the preacher and the church. We started out planning for family to be there but by the time Lynn was finished, we had over a hundred guests.

I can't tell you how I felt when she started down the aisle. I had not seen her or her dress until that moment. She was even more beautiful than our first wedding. Everything went perfect with the ceremony and we had music from the fifties and sixties at the reception, just like the music we loved in the Roundhouse at Reelfoot Lake. We had a couple of young men as our DJs. We rented a large hall with a dance floor and had a full sit-down, catered meal. Our guests ranged in age from less than one year of age to 94 (this was my dear friends Gomer and Goober's Mother. We all call her mama Ruby, one of the wittiest and sweetest ladies you will ever meet.). Lynn had every one of her family members here except for one nephew. She was so overwhelmed that she had her family's support. Some of my family made it. This was indeed a special day we will never forget.

Another special day in my life one of our nieces on her side of the family named one of their sons after me. You know that is such an honor. I hope I can live up to his expectations. This summer they visited over the 4th of July. He is now six years old and his brother is eight. We had a great time together. We fished, drove my tractor, rode my four-wheeler, swam, and played video games. I'm looking forward to next year. As it has always been in my life, there have been so many wonderful things to look forward to.

There are so many stories to tell. I know that as I was writing this book, I have left out so many things I should have written about. Maybe someday I will retire and write another book. No, not when I retire because that may never happen. I love doing things too much to quit.

In life's journey, we have to all realize when we are born God gives each of us a gift and it's up to us to either use our gifts or we lose them. People wonder why some people are so successful and others aren't. It's because they accept God's gifts and use them.

Sometimes it's as simple as taking that first step or standing still. If you don't make the choice to go after your dreams, you will always be the one wondering why others are finding their success. You have to ask yourself how bad you want it. If you're not sure what your gift is, ask God and He will reveal it to you. In life, there are turning points and life-changing events. The most important things in life are God, family, work, and good friends. I have been blessed with all the above beyond belief.

One of our presidents once said, "Be sure you're right, then forge ahead, full-speed, and don't let anyone tell you that you can't do anything you want to do. First, you have to get up, know what you want and go after it. Life is full of twists and turns. It's up to you to straighten them out.

I'm not going to brag, but there are things I need to say. I want to set the record straight. I'm not bragging. If you take anything away from my book, I want you to see where I came from and where life has taken me. I may have been born on the wrong side of the tracks, but I chose not to stay there.

First, I want to make clear that I have had some good jobs and some that were not so good, but I did them. It takes all the pieces to make a puzzle. Without all the pieces, you can't tell what the puzzle is. Life is that way. You and only you can put all the pieces together. Every job I accepted I tried my best to do the best job I could possibly do and I tried to do it right. This type of work ethic will follow you throughout life. However, if you can't be depended on, that will follow through your life as well.

I remember working on the farm when it looked like rain. People would be standing around waiting to see if it was going to rain. My mom would say, "Let's go. We are going to lose a crop waiting for it to rain." In other words, just do it! I was in my forties before I made the first million dollars. After we started our trucking company, we have grossed several million dollars. We created jobs for several people over the last several years. I hope by doing so it helped them. We have always tried to be firm but fair with our employees. That's another thing I've learned in life. You can't please everyone and most of the time the most critical ones are the ones still just standing there.

As I think back, there is so much I'm leaving out of this book. I try hard not to dwell on bad things. I don't like drama. I'm kinda like one of the country singers that thought he had written the perfect song, only to find out it wasn't the perfect country song because he hadn't said anything about mamas, trains, trucks and getting drunk. Well, I haven't written the perfect book either because I left out all that.

I know that sex and drinking and wild parties sell things, but that's not what this is about. It's not about when you're born or when you die. It's what you do in between that counts. Always take care of your friendships and pass along all the good deeds to others. Put others first. Most of the time when you do it turns out whatever they wanted to do was better than what you planned anyway.

Trucking hasn't been easy. There are long hours, you never get away from it. When you go home it's with you, but it has been very rewarding. We have come in contact with so many people over the years, some that have become good friends. We have watched so many of our friends' children grow up who now have families of their own.

Now, if you come away from anything from this book, it's the fact that you can do anything you set out to do if you try hard enough. The grapes are hanging right in front of you. Nobody is going to feed them to you.

Not only do you have to know what gift you have, you also have to have a spouse who will stand by you, support you, and encourage you in everything you do. If I could go from zero to one hundred, you can, too. Life is what you make of it. I have lived both in the South and the North and I have found there are good people everywhere, but I wouldn't trade growing up in the South for all the tea in China. I said earlier that there were things left out that will keep this from being the perfect book. If I put pen to paper again, I will tell you the rest of the story. Hank Williams, Jr. has a song titled "A Country Boy Can Survive." That's me, a Southern country boy. As my friend in Nebraska would say, "You betcha, I am a Southern boy for sure!"

You bet your sweet t e a! Ha!

Made in the USA
Lexington, KY
22 April 2018